Public Speaking and Networking

The Ultimate Guide to Mastering Presentations, Persuasion, Communication, Small Talk and Increasing Your Overall Networking Skills

Contents

Part 1: Public Speaking

Unlock the Secrets to an Emotional and Powerful Presentation, Overcome Fear, and Develop your Confidence, Communication Skills, Social Intelligence, Persuasion Ability, and Charisma

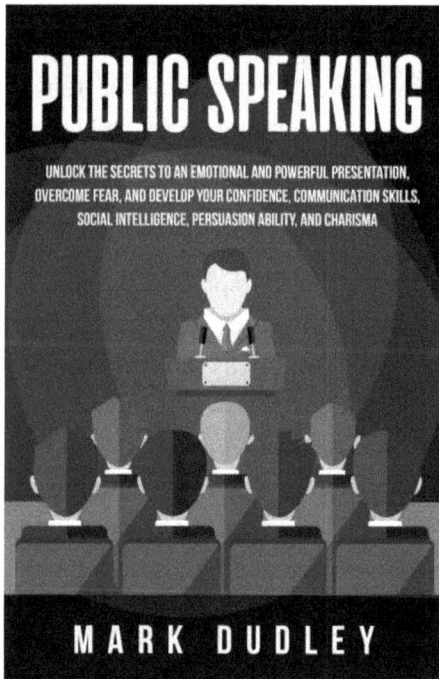

Introduction

You're standing in front of a room full of people. The spotlight is on you. The crowd is waiting in pin-drop silence to hear what you are about to say. Your heart is pounding. Beats of sweat are starting to form across your forehead. You've never felt so paralyzed with nerves and anxiety —this moment, here, when you are faced with the prospect of public speaking.

Do you think you are the only one who feels this way? Guess again.

Not everyone has natural public speaking skills, but it is something everyone can learn and master by practicing the right techniques. Sure, we would all like to be as confident, charming, and self-assured as some of the most renowned public speakers out there— Tony Robbins, Les Brown, Brian Tracey, or the late Steve Jobs (who is still heralded as among the most remarkable storytellers ever to take the stage.) There's no shortage of famous orators out there who have left an impression on the audiences they have addressed.

But what does it take to become like them? How do they make it look so effortless and natural?

The answer is through a lot of hard work, countless practice sessions, plenty of experience, and having the right techniques up their sleeves. In other words, everything that you are about to discover throughout the next few chapters! Feeling at ease on stage is not an impossible dream if you long for it badly enough and put your mind to it. You will become a powerful, emotional public speaker full of confidence, communication skills, ability to persuade with charisma; audiences are not likely to forget you anytime soon.

There are plenty of books on this subject; we are glad you chose this one. Please enjoy!

Chapter 1: Being One with Your Breath

How does the thought of standing in front of a large - or maybe small - group of people make you feel? Standing before them, preparing to give your speech, knowing that all eyes are on you, watching your every move? Are you nervous, or are you perhaps anxious - feeling like you can't breathe? For a lot of people, public speaking is not something that comes naturally, and difficulty in breathing during a speech is just one of the many factors that they need to contend with.

Shortness of breath or feeling like you do not have enough power behind your voice to project or create enough of an impact does not come down to just nerves alone. Of course, if you are nervous, it is going to make it harder to concentrate on your breathing—but even if you are not someone who's prone to stage fight, you could still struggle with the power of projection. Speakers need to be loud and clear enough that the audience in the back of the room can hear them as if they were standing close by.

If you are struggling with breathing, how do you achieve that? First, you need to pinpoint the reasons behind your shortness of breath. Is it a result of the defense mechanism *fight or flight?* Does It stem from social anxiety? Perhaps you are dealing with *glossophobia* (speech anxiety) – a fear of public speaking. If neither of these scenarios applies and you are someone who's comfortable addressing a crowd, then it could be that you are simply not practicing the right breathing techniques or "being one" with your breath.

Often, nervous speakers who struggle with glossophobia experience the following physical symptoms:

- Accelerated or rapid breathing
- Shortness of breath
- Increased or rapid heartbeat
- Dry mouth sensation
- Tense muscles
- Sweaty palms
- Visibly shaking with nervousness
- Feeling anxious

If you experience any of the following at just the thought of making a public speech, you may be dealing with anxiety over public speaking:

- You become distressed, nervous, and visibly awkward and uncomfortable when you must make a speech
- You become distressed when you feel they that you may be teased or criticized - even the very idea is enough to stress you out
- You become distressed when you find yourself in a situation where you are the center of attention
- You become distressed when you feel you are being watched or observed while you are doing something, i.e., giving a speech
- You become distressed when you have to speak in a formal or public situation - even if just a gathering among friends

- You are easily embarrassed to a point where you start blushing and visibly shaking

- You avoid making eye contact for too long - or not at all

All of these factors (and more) play a role in why you are struggling to breathe when tasked with giving a speech or presentation in any kind of context. Some cases of glossophobia could be so extreme that even if you had to conduct a presentation among friends or fellow colleagues whom you see every day, the very idea of being the only one standing up and having to talk is enough to send you into a tailspin. When you struggle even to compose yourself and keep your heart rate beating at an average pace, it is going to impact your ability to project your voice and deliver and speech with the necessary vigor, power, and enthusiasm that you need to make it useful and effective.

The good news is that this does not have to hold you back forever! Even the most nervous speakers out there can still learn a few tricks of the trade. With copious amounts of practice, these can turn you into the impactful public speaker that you have always wanted to be.

The Power of Your Breath

Let's talk about the power of your breath, as well as how crucial this aspect is for your public speaking performance. Here's an example to illustrate this point:

You're in a meeting room at work, and two of your colleagues are about to present. Colleague A and Colleague B are both talking about exactly the same thing, yet only Colleague B seems to stand out. When the other co-workers who were present at that meeting reflect on it, Colleague B seems to prominently feature in their minds and therefore, gets the credit for the presentation. Even though Colleague A was talking about the exact same thing.

Why does this happen? Because Colleague B was doing something different, and the difference was the way he/she *sounded.* Yes, the way that you sound can be the deciding factor that determines whether you were as effective in your presentation as you should have been. Your audience *knows* the difference between someone who sounds nervous and someone who sounds confident. If you have ever been in the audience when a nervous speaker was presenting, you can tell just how they feel through the subtle tremors in their voice. You may believe you are doing a good job of trying to hide just how nervous you really are, but your body language and the way that you sound will be a dead giveaway, even if you appear somewhat composed on the outside.

Try this quick exercise and say this phrase out loud: *"I have something to say."*

Say that once in a firm and confident voice. Now, say it a second time, but this time try imagining you are nervous or afraid when speaking. Record yourself during this exercise and then play it back. Do you hear the difference? You're saying the exact same thing, yet *the way* you say it has a striking contrast. The clear, strong, and confident voice is going to be the one that resonates with you and stands out the most, and this is just why *Colleague B* was memorable while *Colleague A* was not. Which voice do you want your speakers to hear?

Maintaining the right breathing technique can make a world of difference in how you sound when you are giving a speech or presentation. Singers, for example, are a group of people who understand just how much their voice can be affected by the way that they breathe. Some singers take professional vocal training classes to learn how to breathe better so they can project a loud, strong and powerful voice when they sing so every single audience member can hear them as clear as day. Learning how to *be one with your breath* is the key to turning you into a powerful public speaker, someone who is able to command the attention of the audience from the moment you utter the words, *"Hello, and welcome."*

Yet, despite its importance, breathing techniques are *still* the most overlooked aspect when preparing for a speech. You've prepared yourself mentally, carefully reviewed your material, dressed the part, and practiced your speech a dozen times in your head by now. Yet, *did you prepare with the right breathing exercises to help you project your voice on that day?* Most likely not.

If you want to see just what a difference training your voice and breathing can make, there is a **recording** of former United Kingdom Prime Minister Margaret Thatcher which illustrates this perfectly. The former Prime Minister undertook voice lessons when she was elected to her post, and the difference in her speech is remarkable. While some speculators believe that she was making a conscious effort to speak in lower tones (there is **research** to suggest that deeper voices have greater success in politics and business), it is, in fact, her *breathing* that is making the most significant difference. With correct breathing techniques, the former UK Prime Minister's voice sounds decidedly richer and more vibrant—and as a result of that, it automatically seems lower, as well.

The Difference Between Shallow Breathing and Deep Breathing

Breathing occurs so naturally to us that we do not even think about it. Unless we make a conscious, mindful attempt to concentrate on the flow of air that moves in and out of our bodies, chances are we could go through the entire day without even giving our breath a second thought. Breathing is the flow of oxygen traveling from our atmosphere into our lungs, involving carbon dioxide movement from our lungs to outside of our bodies. However, little do we realize that there is a lot more to it than the simple inhale and exhale process. There are specific *breathing techniques* involved which differentiate shallow breathing from deep breathing.

Deep Breathing

Deep breathing also referred to as diaphragmatic breathing, which is when we make full use of our diaphragm, purposefully expanding our lungs to their fullest capacity. This can often be seen as our diaphragms press into our abdomen, causing our bellies to expand outwards.

With deep breathing, the expansion is taking place in our abdomen instead of at the chest or thoracic cavity. This technique is considered a focused technique, one which can prove useful as a cure for certain symptoms we may experience. It is technique requiring concentration because it is not something that we naturally do when we breathe at a regular rate. When we're nervous or anxious, for example, we're encouraged to take deep, focused, measured breaths to help us calm our nerves. Deep breathing is also promoted as a temporary relief from headaches, stress, high blood pressure, anxiety, and even pain. Some women use this measured technique to help them through the labor process.

To breathe in deeply, you would need to focus on drawing air in through your nose and consciously thinking about filling your abdomen area with as much air as possible. You would then focus on holding your breath for at least two seconds before you exhale just as deeply in a controlled measure through your mouth. Not only is this technique useful in situations where you need to calm yourself down, but deep, diaphragmatic breathing also lends power and strength to your voice. Among the benefits that come with this breathing technique are:

- It increases the amount of oxygen that your brain receives because you are breathing in more air

- It helps you stay calm by purposefully slowing down your heart rate, forcing you to concentrate on your breathing instead of your nerves

- Taking in excessive oxygen and expanding your abdomen improves your stance, giving you "power pose" instead of the hunched over, nervous posture that you might otherwise project

- Lends clarity and strength to your voice, which in turn gives you an air of authority

- Gives the appearance of confidence

When combined, these benefits give you the authority, credibility, and believability needed to showcase you as a successful public speaker.

Shallow Breathing

Unlike deep breathing, shallow breathing tends to stop at the chest, rather than travel all the way down to the belly and abdomen. Shallow breathing draws only minimal amounts of air into your lungs, moving only the chest area during the breath. Much of the time, this breathing occurs involuntarily, and most people are unaware of this breathing technique. In fact, this is the kind of breathing that we employ every day for our survival; we do not even stop to think about it. As you are reading this right now, consider which type of breathing you are employing. That slow, even pace is your shallow breathing.

Shallow breathing can occur in other instances, like hyperventilation - that even rapid breathing when you are feeling particularly scared, nervous, or anxious. Your breath quickens and gives the appearance of "rapid" breathing because very little air is traveling in and out of your lungs, which causes your breath to quicken. This type of breathing could also be symptomatic of other conditions, including pneumonia, shock, asthma, panic, stress, and other possible health conditions associated with the lungs. The danger with shallow breathing for a prolonged period is that it could quickly lead to carbon dioxide building up in your body, which in turn leads to an increase in the acidity levels in your bloodstream.

If you were to watch a newborn baby's breathing, you'd notice that – instinctively - they often employ the deep breathing technique, providing maximum benefits for their body. Watching them, you'll notice their chest and abdomen rise and fall visibly, an indication that deep breathing is happening. For adults, however, this type of breathing is no longer done instinctively. In general, most people tend to be shallow or thoracic breathers, shifting over time as we grow and acclimatize to the everyday stressors and triggers in our environment.

Shallow breathing is *not beneficial* for your body because it keeps the body in a cyclical stress state. Your stress is causing you to breathe in a shallow manner, *and your shallow breathing,* in turn, is causing you to stress out. Since chronic stress is linked to shallow breathing, getting stuck in a prolonged period with this breathing pattern can have serious consequences on your health. When faced with a public speaking situation, shallow breathing can aggravate your stress levels, causing full-blown panic attacks, dry mouth, difficulty breathing, and even be a precursor for potential cardiovascular problems.

How Proper Breathing Techniques Affect the Sound of Your Voice

The right breathing techniques help you feel calmer and more relaxed, resulting in your voice becoming steadier, stronger, and more compelling. Public speaking is a situation that can challenge you as a person on several levels, yet at the same time, it can be a deeply rewarding, satisfying experience. You only need to observe motivational speakers in action in order to see how true this is. Nothing is more rewarding or exciting than speaking on a subject that you are deeply passionate about - a subject you believe in so much that you want to spread the word and share what you know! The most successful, high-profile, and inspirational speakers in the world have shaped, inspired, and changed the lives of millions with a powerful speech. Leaders have rallied together nations and spurred them to action with the help of a compelling, emotional, and impactful speech.

If you are wondering what the secret is to become a confident speaker, here's the answer: *You are doing it already.* You are *breathing.* Now, you need to learn to be one with your breath and employ the power of deep, diaphragmatic breathing as your most empowering public speaking tool. The phrase, *"Take a deep breath,"* is not just a calming axiom; it is an actual tool that you can use to your advantage when you do it right. Every speaker - motivational or otherwise - that you see on stage moving crowds and leaving a powerful, lasting impression behind *is doing it with the help of deep breathing techniques.*

Regardless of your gender or how powerful your voice is right now, everyone can benefit from certain, specific exercises that you can practice at home and remember to use when you are in front of a crowd.

> • **1-2-3-Breathe** - Breathing can be as easy as counting *1-2-3.* Start your deep breathing practice sessions off by mindfully counting *1-2-3* as you slowly and deliberately inhale, and then count *1-2-3* again as you slowly and deliberately exhale. *1-2-3* breathe in, *1-2-3* breathe out. Involve all your senses as you do this. If it helps, combine it with a positive phrase or mantra that helps you feel empowered. As you breathe in and count *1-2-3,* repeat a phrase that helps you stay calm and focused. Do this before a speech, and even during moments of your speech when you may be struggling to feel calm.

> • **Stand Tall, Back Straight** - Not to the point you feel uncomfortable but stand straight and tall, so your shoulders are back, and your posture is great. Adopt a stance where your feet are positioned shoulder-width apart, with your weight equally distributed. If you are practicing this at home, raise your arms over your head while you breathe deeply and inhale. As you exhale, slowly lower your arms down to your sides in a controlled manner -do not rush it. Keep your shoulders back the entire time, not hunched. When you are in front of a crowd and giving your speech, the shoulder-width apart and shoulders back stance is the best posture you can adopt. Not only does this allow you to breathe deeply when you need to, standing tall also gives you the appearance of being a confident speaker.

Hand on Belly and Chest - Place one hand on your stomach where your belly button is and take the other hand and place it on your chest. As you breathe deeply, pay close attention to the hand that is moving. When most people breathe, their chest moves up and down; to practice deep breathing, you must keep your chest steady and focus on moving your abdominal area instead. The hand that is on your belly should be the one that makes the most movement now, not the hand on your chest. Practice this at home several times and even several minutes prior to your speech to help you get into a relaxed state of mind.

• **Let Your Breath Support Your Words -** After practicing with a few deep breaths, try speaking, allowing your breath to support the words that come out of your mouth. For this exercise, pick a sentence you would like to try practicing. As you speak, slowly exhale while you do, and let your voice resonate with its full, vibrant, and supported sound. To begin, start by slowly exhaling as you say *1 - 2 - 3 - 4 - 5,* and then do it again except this time, imagine you were giving a speech and say, *"Hello, my name is..."* Slowly exhale while you speak, noticing the difference in the way that your voice sounds when it is accompanied by a deep breath.

Exercises to Improve Vocal Strength

These exercises are designed to help you rely on your abdominal muscles to strengthen the sound of your voice. As you practice these exercises, you want to make sure that you can hear yourself breathing in and out as you do. Aim to do these exercises at least once a day, twice a week, or as often as you feel you need it.

• Start by lying down flat on your back in a comfortable position. You want to be sure that you are comfortable because the next step is putting a book on top of your stomach. If you are not comfortable using a book, placing your hands on top of your stomach works just as well.

• Now, as you breathe in from your mouth, feel the way the book (or your hands) is rising. As you exhale, feel it lower. This step should feel natural and effortless. Practice this for several minutes.

• The second step begins with you sitting upright in a chair. Keep your shoulders back, sit up tall, and place one hand on your stomach.

• Repeat the same breathing motions you did when you were on your back, and this time observe the movement of your hand as you feel your stomach moving in and out with each breath. It helps to sit in front of a mirror and watch yourself doing this.

• After a couple of practice sessions, try saying "hmmm" as you release your breath through your nose. You want to do this deliberately and "feel" the vibration around your nose as you do. The "hmmm" sound should be resonating from your nose, not your throat.

• Next, move onto saying actual words instead of "hmmm." Start with a short word like "up." To do this right, it has to sound as though you are saying "hup," instead of "up." That's how you know you are doing it right. Once you are comfortable, progress to longer sentences and words, like "Up, one ...up, two... up, three" and continue all the way up to 10. Remember to take a deep breath after each phrase.

• Once you are comfortable with this exercise, move on to longer phrases, like you would with a speech. Say, "I'm going to buy some food," and practice saying it with the breathing techniques you learned above. Remember that the breath should be coming in from your mouth, and the air is released as you speak out loud.

These exercises help you remain conscious of allowing the air to flow from your abdomen for maximum power instead of coming from the thoracic area. As you continue to practice, it begins to feel easier and more natural until eventually, you'll be able to do this effortlessly in any speech or presentation.

Bonus Tip: Don't Forget to Smile!

When you are feeling nervous, sometimes the best thing to do smile through it all. Smiling not only brings people together, but it also makes you appear more approachable, and it triggers emotional changes in the body, too. A good dose of laughter triggers endorphins in your brain, and it is just what you need to help you feel relaxed when you need it most—*right before* your public speaking session. The next time you feel particularly anxious over an upcoming presentation, try laughing – *genuinely* - over a funny thought, joke or memory and see what a difference it makes. Even better, try enlisting the help of a friend or colleague to help lighten the mood.

Chapter 2: Prepping Your Mind, Body, Soul, and Voice

Public speaking: you either love it, hate it, or are completely terrified by the very thought of it. There's certainly no shortage of advice out there, telling you how to overcome and prepare for a presentation despite your fears—but they may only overwhelm you more. Have you heard the old adage about picturing everyone in the audience in their underwear? That's not going to help – not when your mind is racing a mile a minute, wishing you were anywhere else but on stage or in front of a room addressing a crowd. Advice will come and go. Some will work well for you, while others do not help at all. There is only one tried and true approach to public speaking that continues to hold true: *you must prepare mentally, physically, emotionally, and vocally* for what's ahead.

Feeling tense or nervous before a presentation or a speech is normal. Even the best speakers out there occasionally experience moments where they feel butterflies in the pit of their stomach. Being nervous is not uncommon. To combat the nervousness, you must prepare yourself mentally and physically – through exercise. You might hear the term "loosening up" thrown about quite a bit, and that refers to the exercises which help you feel more confident and prepared the stage.

The exercises that you are about to work through right now are ideal for anyone who could use a little help relaxing before their big speech. Whether you are a beginning or seasoned speaker, these exercises are designed to help you maintain the calm and focus that you need to get through your presentation.

Physical Exercises to Loosen Up the Body

Stiff and tense muscles are a hindrance to calmness when you are in front of your audience. When you are not relaxed, your body is going to show, and your listeners will sense your discomfort. Try the following physical exercises to get rid of some of that tension in your muscles:

- **Start at the Neck and Shoulders** - Neck and shoulder roll exercises are great for relieving pressure and tension in the upper body. Especially since the neck and shoulder area is where we typically feel most of the strain. The expression *"feeling like a weight has been lifted off my shoulders"* perfectly illustrates what significant impact stress can have on your body. When you are standing for your speech, these tense muscles can make you feel extremely uncomfortable, making it hard to focus on your points. These exercises are easy enough to do anywhere you are, and you should certainly do these a couple of times prior to your speech. Roll your head from one side to the other, moving it in a slow, deliberate circular fashion. Think of it as drawing a circle in the air, but with your head. Roll your shoulders forward, also in a circular fashion like you are attempting to draw a circle in the air. Do this a couple of times, and then switch and rotate them backward.

- **Stretching Out Your Arms** - Take your shoulder relief one step further by stretching out your arms. We use our arms a lot during a presentation or a speech and having stiff or painful muscles can hinder your gesturing. This, in turn, could affect the power and delivery of your speech when the proper gestures or hand signals do not accompany the point you make. Stretching your arm muscles before a speech can loosen the strain you feel, and significantly improve your body language when you are not in such discomfort. Stretch out your arms in front of you as far as you can, holding the position for several minutes. It should feel really good when you release that stretch. Repeat this move, stretching them behind you, and to the side, too.

• **Do the Twist** - Not the dance move, but waist stretches instead to relieve the pressure from your torso and lower back area. When you are standing during your speech, the last thing you want is to be distracted by the pain in your lower back or torso area, which might even affect your posture and the way that you stand. Remember, posture and stance are important in delivering a confident persona to your audience. These exercises are also easily performed anywhere on the go. Stand with your feet slightly apart, place your hands on your hips and rotate your waist from side to side, once again attempting to draw a circle in the air with your body. Rotate from left to right, alternating from right to left.

Vocal Exercises to Help You Prepare

Now that your body is relieved from some of that strain, it is time to move on to vocal exercises to help you prepare for your upcoming presentation. Vocal exercises are important to ensure that your anxiety does not translate through your voice. A powerful speaker sounds confident, and your voice needs to be strong and steady enough to command the attention of every single person in that room.

• **Start with the "Shush"** - This is where you begin your deep breathing techniques. Relax your shoulders, pull them back, stand up tall, and place your hands on your belly. Now, take deep, measured breaths, pushing your stomach in with your hands. Exhaling and pushing out all the air you just took in, say *"SHHHHHHHHHHHHHHH," as* loudly as you can, keeping your shoulders down as you do. If it helps, picture yourself as a librarian or teacher who is shushing your students.   This should help further relax your body and prepare you for the next few vocal exercises.

• **Trill the Tongue** - Yes, it is just what it sounds like. You're about to warm up your tongue, too, so it is nice and relaxed when you are ready to give your speech. Trilling the tongue involves a simple maneuver of rolling your tongue as fast as you can in your mouth. What you are basically trying to do is force the air in your mouth to go past your tongue is such a fast manner that your tongue feels like it is vibrating almost. Linguists call this little exercise the "rolling of the R's."

• **The Hum** - Humming is the quickest way to relax your vocal cords and warm them up in preparation for your presentation.   The vibrating sensation loosens your vocal cords. Start with a long *hmmmmmmm*, and keep the sound going for as long as possible.   Then, try doing it without pressing your lips together, keeping your jaws, cheeks, lips, and mouth nice and relaxed as you do. Finally, try humming in ascending and descending tones, increasing and lowering your voice as you do.

• **Enunciate It** - Your final vocal exercises are going to be pronouncing and articulating your words as clearly as possible. Pronounce each *T* and *P* sound as distinctly as possible.   Choose several sentences to practice with, enunciating each word in that sentence, opening your mouth wide so that it seems as though you are speaking in an exaggerated manner - which you are.

• **Do the Tongue Twist** - Instead of twisting your waist this time, you are going to now focus on twisting the tongue instead. Tongue twisters are great to help you practice your speech, avoiding the dreaded mumbling, speaking too quickly or even "swallowing" parts of your sentences or words. Those downfalls will kill your presentation. Your audience *must* understand what you are saying, and tongue twisters offer the ideal solution. These twisters force you to repeat similar sound patterns; saying them out loud during the exercises forces you to focus on what you are saying. If you have ever had to say a tongue twister before, you'll know just how much concentration goes into getting the sentence out just right to avoid your words coming out garbled.

Mental Exercises for Improved Concentration During Your Speech

Our brains are fascinating: they are capable of experiencing many emotions, brainstorming, mentally juggling multiple thoughts and solutions, sourcing memories at any given time, and more. Often, we mistake the human brain and *the mind*, thinking that they are the same thing. Nothing, however, could be further from the truth.

The brain is an organ, functioning much like the rest of our organs do. The mind, on the other hand, is a representation of our emotions and thoughts. Put differently, the brain is the organ which houses our mind. Just how our minds work has been the subject of many areas of study, including psychology, neuroscience, and human philosophy. What makes you tick? What's going on in my head? Why do we come up with the thoughts that we do? One of the ways in which the human mind works is that it is driven by the *information at hand.*

Since our mind is where our emotions take place, the mind is responsible for how we feel *before* and *during* the speeches that we make. To give your best performance at every presentation you make, you need to be in the right frame of mind. A mind that is overrun with emotions of fear, worry, and anxiety cannot concentrate on the task and hand. The ability to stay focused during your speech is going to be the difference between a presentation that was "alright", and one that was "outstanding."

If becoming an outstanding public speaker is where you want to be, then you need to start training your mind with the right mental exercises to help you hold onto those powers of concentration, especially when under intense pressure. Mental warm-ups prepare you for getting into the "zone"; the following exercises will be what you need to help strengthen your focus and concentration.

Before starting, you must find a place that is free of distractions. Find a space that is quiet and comfortable, where you can easily settle into as you start working on your concentration levels. It is very important that you remain comfortable throughout the session; if not, you'll become easily distracted by any discomfort, making it hard for you to get started off on the right foot.

- **Find an Object of Focus -** Once you are in your quiet zone, find an object you can focus on and place it in front of you. Begin focusing only on your object, starting with small intervals of time, ranging between 3 to 5- minutes. Maintain your focus throughout that period, concentrating on nothing except the object in front of you. Once you are able to maintain this prolonged period of concentration without distraction, slowly increase the time increments. Bring it up to 10-minutes, then 15-minutes and so on. Train yourself over time to increase your concentration for longer and longer periods.

- **Creating a To-Do List for Distractions -** It may sound strange, but it works. Our minds are prone to wandering, and you will find odd thoughts crossing your mind when you least expect it. Instead of leaving these random thoughts to their own devices, try writing them down whenever they pop into your head, especially if they are concerns you possess over speaking in public. Throughout the day as you go about your daily routine, when a random thought pops up, make a note of it by writing it down so you can come back to it again at a later time. Write it down and then immediately put that thought out of your mind and return to the task you were doing before that thought interfered. This is also a great exercise that trains you to snap back into your focused mode whenever you are briefly distracted.

• **Being Mindful Throughout the Day** - Instead of going through the motions, try being mindful of everything that you do throughout your daily routine. We do a lot each day without giving much -if any- thought to the task. Remember our breathing? Now that you are working on increasing your mental focus, being mindful throughout the day is a useful exercise to enhance that focus. Be mindful of everything, even simple things like putting on your socks, brushing your teeth, or eating your meals. Being mindful of what you are doing and of your surroundings is going to train you to concentrate on being present and observant. It forces you to pay attention to what is essential.

More Specific Techniques, Exercises, and Warm-Ups – Discreet and Easy

Even the most nervous public speaker can perform certain exercises to help them feel more comfortable before a big speech or presentation. It might not completely get rid of the butterflies in your stomach, but it does help you feel a lot more composed and in control. Besides preparing your material, rehearsing it several times, practicing your breathing, and working on your vocal exercises, your body language is another factor that must be considered. Body language can make a significant impression on your audience, so you'll need to make sure yours is sending the right message!

Your body language is going to tell your audience what they need to know about you as a speaker. Are you convincing? Are you confident? Or are you so nervous that you can't wait to get it over with? Are you rushing through your speech because you want to get off the stage? Your confidence as a public speaker is going to in the way you carry yourself, not just by the words coming out of your mouth.

Exercise #1: Working on Your Power Pose

There is evidence that adopting a power pose stance can actually help you feel stronger and effective. U.S-based social psychologists Dana Carney, Andy Yap, and Amy Cuddy put forth this **theory** in 2011, claiming that power poses help lower cortisol and raise testosterone levels.

In other words, standing in a power pose drops your stress levels and raises your feelings of dominance. Pretending to feel more powerful eventually leads to feelings of confidence. To practice this move, stand tall in front of a mirror with your feet shoulder-width apart and shoulders back, adopting good posture. Rest your hands on your hips (like Superman!) Hold this pose for several minutes until you start to feel more confident. When you are on stage or in front of the room, giving your presentation, imitate the power pose, tilting your body towards different areas in front of you. This forward-tilt towards different areas of the room helps your audience feel connected and included.

Exercise #2: Good Eye Contact

There may be a lot of people in the room, but you still need to try and maintain good eye contact with as many audience members as possible, even when you are feeling nervous. Eye contact with the audience helps foster a connection, making it seem as though you are speaking directly to them. This helps an audience feel valued and important, making it more likely to listen and pay attention during your speech. Think about the speaker who merely reads from his notes and barely glances up at the audience; his listeners will lose interest soon.

Good eye contact also fosters that element of trust, since eye contact avoidance is notoriously linked to lying or being dishonest. Practice good eye contact in your daily interactions. Whenever you find yourself having a conversation with someone, hold the connection for no more than 10 seconds before breaking away quickly and then resuming eye contact. Anything more than ten seconds can be interpreted as intimidating.

When you are addressing a crowd, hold eye contact with one audience member for no more than 4 seconds before you move on to the next person so that it does not seem as though you are focused on just one person alone. Your eye contact during a presentation should take on a "Z" formation. For example, you start by looking at the person sitting in the far-left seat. Then, your eyes should travel to the person on the right, sitting in the same row. Then, move forward to the front left, and then the front right. Picture it like you are drawing the letter "Z" through your audience with your eyes.

Exercise #3: Move and Pace

Standing stiffly and rooted to one spot on the stage is the worst thing you could do as a public speaker. You're not showing strong leadership or confidence when you do that. You may be an expert on your subject, but you are not going to convince anyone unless your body language shows it. Moving around the stage shows confidence, and it gives the impression that you are speaking to everyone in the audience. Taking charge and owning the space around you is something a strong leader does. That is the signal you want to send your audience.

When practicing your speech at home, imagine you are in front of your audience, working on your timing and pacing. Avoid moving and pacing too much, though, because that is going to be distracting. Ideally, you should wait for 3-minutes before moving from one area to the other. Practice this at home in front of a mirror if possible, so that in your real performance, your movements seem effortless and natural. Another element is *timing your movements* so that your movements are in sync with subject changes. Each time you ask your audience a question, or creating emphasis on a point, move forward towards the crowd.

When using a mirror in practice, be sure you can always see yourself when you move around. Likewise, on speech day, your audience should always be within your line of vision. Avoid turning away or having your back turned to any part of the audience—this leads to feelings of disconnection. When you talk to someone in person, you will not turn your back on them; aside from being rude, it makes them feel excluded and unimportant. That's the same approach you want to use when you are addressing any crowd.

Exercise #4: Facial Expressions

While your audience may be observing your body language, they will also be closely watching your facial expressions, assessing whether you are genuine or not. Listeners respond better to a speaker who is expressive, whose face tells the story in a powerful way. This exercise, once again, works best in front of a mirror where you can see what you are doing. Observe the facial expressions you make as you rehearse your speech. Does your expression match the message you are trying to convey?

Exercise #5: Observing Your Mannerisms

Sometimes we do not see or know our own mannerisms until someone else points them out. Mannerisms are the habits that rise to the surface when we're nervous, and these can be distracting, causing your listeners discomfort. That discomfort, in turn, may keep them distracted and unable to focus on your message. Fiddling and fidgeting, for example, are nervous mannerisms. Others include excessive gestures, putting your hands in your pockets, crossing your arms in front of your chest, and even using too many filler words like "umm."

To overcome this, record yourself when practicing at home, playing it back, and carefully watching your own performance. Have a friend or family member watch it with you so they can give you their feedback on what mannerisms they think you need to discard. Make a list of your mannerisms, and work on dumping them as you continue with several more practice runs of your speech. Record yourself each time to see if there is any improvement.

Chapter 3: Two Power P's – Pace and Pause

In order to deliver a presentation that is going to leave an impact long after you are finished, it is not enough to just stand in front of your audience and deliver the material you have prepared. Facts, numbers, and interesting revelations are good—but there is still more that needs to be done if you want your crowd to keep talking about your speech long after it is over.

For an effective presentation, you'll need to incorporate the *6-P System* as part of your design and delivery:

> • *Preparation (Before)* - The very first *P* of your process is preparation, which takes place *before* the speech. In this section, you need to think about who your audience is, what you are going to be talking about, how this information addresses their concerns, and how it is going to affect or benefit them. Which of your main talking points do you want them to recall the most?

> • *Planning (Before)* - After the *Preparation,* next comes the planning. Here, the questions to be addressed are what your introduction and conclusion should be, and how you intend

to structure your presentation. How do you include all the most vital information in the most concise manner? How much visual reinforcement should you include in your presentation? How long should your presentation last? How many slides should you include in your PowerPoint, if you are using one?

• *Practice (Before)* - Practice as many times as you can before your presentation. Practice at home, in your car, and any time you have a free moment to spare. Practice in front of your family, your friends, even in front of a camera. Watch recordings of yourself, seek feedback from family and friends, and look for areas of improvement you can tweak.

• *Project (During)* - For your speech to be effective, you need to remember the next *"P"* in the process, which is to *project* your voice as much as possible. You need to be loud enough to be heard, but not *too loud* that you sound like you are yelling. This is where the breathing techniques come in play, and you must practice enough for deep breathing to become second nature.

• *Pace (During)* - To allow your message to resonate and sink in with your audience, you need to pace yourself during your speech. Incorporating difference paces during your speech helps to alleviate monotony and boredom. During the exciting, interesting parts of your speech, speeding it up a little can create a sense of excitement and anticipation in your audience, keeping them on the alert for what's coming next. Slowing the rate of your pace at certain points in your speech helps to build a sense of importance surrounding your information.

• *Pause (During)* - Closely linked with pace, these last two *P's* work in tandem to create a maximum impact during your presentation. Pausing during the parts of your presentation (i.e., when delivering your most important information) gives emphasis to your points. This provides your listeners with the needed time to allow the information to sink in before you move onto your next key point. Some of the best speakers out there are at the top of their game because they know just how to pace their speech while skillfully utilizing pauses to make the most out of their delivery.

Out of the *6-P's* listed above, pay the closest attention to the final two.

Using Pace and Pause to Your Advantage

Knowing when to pace and pause during your speech - and using them to your advantage to emphasize certain points - will guarantee that your speech will be exciting and enticing. When you keep your audience guessing, they will be intrigued, hanging onto your every word without even trying. Without the power of *pace and pause,* you could have the most riveting subject in the world, but that won't be enough to stifle those yawns or stop your listeners from zoning out.

The Drawbacks of Being a Fast Talker

For your audience to sit up and pay attention, you need to be the one who sets the pace. You're the commander of the room now, and it is up to you to execute the perfect delivery. Many new or inexperienced public speakers often struggle at the beginning with poor control over their pace, mostly because they are nervous, and it shows. Many new speakers often talk too fast, not pausing enough during their speech, which only makes them sound even *more nervous* than they already are. It's hard for your audience to pay attention when they are not given enough time to process what you are saying. How can they, when you are rushing through your speech from one point to the next?

When you rush, it is clear that you have no control over your emotions and that your nerves are getting the best of you. And yes, your audience will see this clearly, as well. Talking too fast forces your audience to work even harder to try and understand what you are saying. Bear in mind: your listeners have come with the expectation of *not having to work hard to listen.* To them, you are the one doing all the work as the presenter. Their job is just to sit there and listen – and they expect it to be an easy job! As soon as they have to exert themselves trying to absorb what you are saying, it won't be long before they tune you out; it is just too much work.

The beauty of speech is about connecting with others. You've been given an opportunity to connect with a group of people all at once, but that becomes hard to do when they can't understand you.

There are other negatives from failing to pace yourself during your speech:

> • Your audience assumes that you are nervous and lack confidence, hurrying as much as possible to finish and get off the stage.

> • You will lack clarity and volume, since talking too quickly won't allow you to take in the necessary air that you need to help your voice project loud and clear.

> • Your diction becomes compromised. Talking too fast does not give your tongue enough time to keep up with your mind, and as a result, important consonants and vowels can be lost. When this happens, the essence of your message is no longer well-received by your audience.

> • Fast-talking causes confusion when your audience can't keep up. Remember that you may understand what you are saying, but that does not mean that they do. Trying to win over your audience is going to be much harder to do when they find your speech confusing.

> • You run the risk of having your audience view you negatively. Your credibility is at risk when you appear impatient, perhaps even aggressive. Additionally, talking fast shows that you lack empathy for your listener, failing to

take their feelings into consideration. Not every listener processes information the same way, and some might need a bit more time than others. Talking too fast shows you have little regard for their needs, that you are only thinking about yourself and getting your speech over with.

As a speaker, learning to pace yourself is going to be one of your greatest assets. True, you may be nervous and probably can't wait to get off the stage and retreat out of the spotlight, but you shouldn't let your audience know that. Pace and pause are masterful public speaking techniques that only a handful of great speakers have managed to accomplish. You can learn to hone these skills, too.

Learning to pause during a speech affords several benefits, yet it continues to remain one of the most overlooked public speaking techniques. This is likely because nerves often win out at the end of the day. When emotions run high, it is hard to concentrate on anything else. Here's what happens when you learn to pause during your speeches effectively:

- Researcher Brigitte Zellner notes in her research that pausing helps your audience better understand you and that the communication process becomes a lot more intelligible as a result. Zellner references even further research by Grosjean and Deschamps (1975), which points out that complex communicative tasks require more pausing. According to Zellner, when pauses occur during communication, a great deal of improvement can be seen in terms of speech comprehension. In other words, since your audience is not going to have the benefit of reading bullet points, bold, italics or punctuation, it is up to you to "create this" in your speech through your pauses and paces.

- Pauses allow your speech to sound more polished, cohesive, coherent, and professional—instead of filling up that time with filler words of no value. It also gives you time, as the speaker, to think about your next talking points, and allows your mind to catch up with your mouth.

• Further research indicates that pauses can effectively convey emotions, especially when the pauses are well-timed. Depending on what you say, your pauses are going to vary based on whether you are trying to convey happiness, enthusiasm, frustration, or any other kind of emotion. For pauses to be used authentically, you need to imagine you are speaking to your audience the way that you would with a family member or a friend.

• If you need help controlling the overall pace of your delivery, pauses are the way to do it. Your audience can only absorb information at a certain rate, and when you pace yourself and pause, you are allowing your rate to match the listening capabilities of the majority of your audience. Research shows that during a speech, three types of pauses tend to occur. Brief pauses (1/4 of a second), medium pauses (up to one second) and long pause of over one second's duration. Short

Pausing allows you to conduct the deep breathing techniques you need to take in more air, which allows your voice to adjust and be ready to project in a steady, clear manner once you start speaking again.

• Pauses allow time for reflection, and when your audience is given a chance to mull over what you have told them, this increases their engagement rates during the question and answer portion of the presentation.

The following techniques are meant to help you nail the right pace and know when to pause for effect so that your speech packs the powerful punch that you hoped for. Do it right, and your pauses during your speech will seem so effortless—and your audience won't be consciously aware of it.

- **Don't Memorize Your Content** - The likelihood of you rushing through your speech is greater when you memorize your facts. The key is to *understand* your subject and know your material so well that you do not need to memorize your content word-for-word.

- **Break It into Chunks.** Take a look at your speech and see where you can break it off into smaller sections or chunks. Reading your speech aloud a few times will help you observe which sections you could plan for your pauses to make it sound more natural.

- **Practice with A Metronome** - There's a useful app for just about anything these days, including practicing your speech. Metronomes can be great tools that help you practice your pace, allowing you to adjust your tempo accordingly as you begin to get a better feel of how fast or how slow you are speaking.

- **Stretching Out Your Vowels** - Non-English speakers use this technique to help them slow down and remain focused on what they say. For this exercise to work, you need to take your time pronouncing your vowels as clearly as possible (but not too slow to the point where you begin to sound unnatural).

- **Fight the Urge to Rush** - When you are nervous, there is going to be a little voice in your head that keeps telling you to *"hurry up!"* so you can get out of there as soon as possible. You're going to have to work very hard to tune that voice out. You worked hard on your presentation, and you know you have got some great material and fantastic benefits for your listeners. You should give them the opportunity to absorb the essence of your message fully and fighting the urge to rush is how you do it. Slow down, take a step back, breathe, count to five, and then resume.

-

How Do I Tell If I'm Speaking Too Quickly?

To you, your speech rate might be just perfect, but that is because you are so used to the way that you speak, you do not see anything wrong with it. Ask a stranger, however, and they might have a completely different view of the way that you talk. In your mind, you might believe that you are adopting the perfect pace, but to your listener, you could be outdistancing their ability to keep up.

Determining your speech rate (the speed at which you speak) is a very useful piece of information. This speed is calculated based on the number of words that are spoken in a minute. General speed rate guidelines dictate the following classifications of speech rates:

> • **Slow speech rate:** *Less than 110 Words-per-Minute (WPM)*
>
> • **Conversational speech rate:** Somewhere between *120 WPM to 150 WPM*
>
> • **Fast speech rate:** *Exceeds 160 WPM*

Examples of a conversational speech rate are podcasters and radio hosts, who, on average, speak anywhere from 150-160 WPM. In case you need an example of how to sound natural or conversational during a speech, it might be helpful to listen to several podcasts beforehand. You might also find it helpful to watch several videos on speeches by Barack Obama, Amy Tan, or Steve Jobs – all exemplary role models of well-paced public speakers.

An example of how you *do not* want to speak during a presentation is like an auctioneer or a commentator. On average, they utter anywhere from 250-400 WPM, which is much too fast and completely inappropriate for an effective presentation.

Chapter 4: Have You Been Listening to Your Tone?

Speeches—they can either be great or terrible. Even the most well-put-together presentations (or even ones at a mediocre level) can end up being terrible on the actual day of the presentation. When that happens, there is usually one reason for it—*it is uninspiring and boring.* You could have done everything right up to that point. You prepared. You practiced. You even did your breathing exercises and vocal warm-ups. Yet, the presentation was uninspiring and dull because it wasn't delivered in an interesting manner. That alone makes a difference, and you either end up with a room full of attentive, alert and engaged listeners—or a room full of sleepy, zoned-out listeners who are idly checking their phones and counting the minutes until your speech is over.

How Using Varied Vocal Tones Can Make a Difference

Monotonous speakers tend to be the dullest and most uninspiring kind; nobody wants to sit and listen for half an hour or more to someone who speaks with little to no variation in their tone of voice. Varying your vocal tone not only engages your audience, but it also energizes your words through the emotional inflections used in your speaking. Before this can happen, *you* need to be emotionally invested and interested in what you are talking about. If you are not passionate about your topic, then you are not the right person to speak in public about that subject. Motivational speakers like Les Brown and Tony Robbins can move audiences and strike an emotional chord with them *because* they believe in what they preach. They're passionate about their topics, and this passion shines through every word of every sentence that they speak.

Giving a speech does not mean you should sound stiff and rigid. In fact, you should *let* your audience witness the full range of emotions that you feel when you talk about certain aspects of your speech. When the statistics leave you feeling angry or frustrated, let them know it. When you are excited about a new revelation, show them how you feel and allow them to share in the excitement, too. Be animated from the moment you walk onto the stage and use your emotional inflections to help you tell a story with your speech.

Go back and review Chapter 1. In the example of Colleague A and Colleague B, one was more memorable than the other even though they were presenting on the same subject. The difference was due to the *way* each colleague presented their points. You could be saying all the right things, but if you do not say it in the right *way,* it is not going to be effective!

The Way You Say It Matters

Consider this scenario: You've noticed your work buddy with a miserable, grumpy, and unhappy expression on his face. He's frowning, his arms are folded across his chest, and everything about his body language is screaming out loud for you to back off. Yet, you do what any concerned colleague would do, venturing to ask him if he's okay. He responds, "I'm fine," but his smile is forced, and his tone is clipped. From the way he responds, you instinctively know that everything is *not fine*, despite what he is saying. It clear that his body language does not match his message.

It does not matter what words are coming out of your mouth—it is your *tone of voice* that determines how well your message is received by your audience. The inflection of your voice, the volume at which you speak, your pace, and your tone are all the elements that come together and contribute to the effectiveness of your speech. Dr. Albert Mehrabian, a professor and psychologist renowned for his work and publications on verbal and nonverbal communication and its relative importance, understood what a significant role our voices play in our speech.

Dr. Mehrabian created what is now known as the *7-38-55 Rule for Personal Communication.* Using this formula, a communication that is going to be 100% successful is going to come down to how well you follow the formula. In this rule, 7% of communication comes from your words, while 38% is the way that you convey these words, and the remaining 55% is the body language that is used when delivering your message. The fact that 38% belongs to the way we say things is a big indicator of just how important tone of voice is in the communication process.

The tone of voice boils down to attitude. Your voice is not going to change. It's the way that you *speak* that is going to alter the effectiveness of your speech. Give a presentation when you have had a particularly rough day, and in a bad mood, then your speech won't be nearly as impactful; your heart is not in it. When your heart's not in it, your tone will be the dead giveaway. Forced passion and cheerfulness will never sound as convincing as the real deal. If you haven't been having much luck with your speeches so far, this might be one reason why!

Monotony is Boredom

Monotonous or unvaried speech is not just boring to listen to, but it also makes a speaker sound disinterested in their own presentation. Your audience might also assume that you are not confident about your own thoughts or ideas, and that is why you sound as if you were doing nothing more than reading from a script. Monotony has no compassion, no emotion, and no feeling behind it—which is why it does very little to inspire your audience, making for a terrible speech presentation. No audience member wants to sit through all of that and walk away feeling like they got nothing beneficial out of the session.

Monotonous speech delivery is an all-too-common pitfall for many speakers – and one that can easily be avoided. It's not just new speakers that fall prey, seasoned speakers still struggle with shaking off old habits. Nothing kills communication like a monotone voice, and you will lose your audience within the first five minutes of the speech if you do not learn to liven up your speaking voice.

It is *impossible* for your audience to maintain an interest in what you are saying if you are boring. You've probably had to sit through a few less-than-thrilling presentations in your lifetime, so you'll understand just how hard it can be. Struggling to maintain focus when the speaker is doing nothing to encourage the situation can only result in one thing: you tune them out quickly. As the speaker, once again, your message has failed to make the impact that you hoped it would, and you can't quite figure out why.

Here's a couple of other problems that monotone delivery presents:

> • Your audience perceives you as dull and uninteresting when you sound like you are droning on and on about a bunch of memorized facts.

> • Monotone voices are often perceived to be shifty and untrustworthy because there is no emotion behind the message.

> • Your audience does not see you as upbeat or cheerful, and if you are presenting on a subject with good news in it, your voice is going to contradict the message that you are trying to send.

> • There are inconsistencies between what you say and your body language, which makes you appear untrustworthy or shady.

Thankfully, it is not the end of the world if you do happen to struggle with monotony and a lack of variety in your vocal tones when presenting. The exercises listed below are designed to help you get more out of your vocals, so you will be saying the following sentences differently each time.

Exercise #1

Say the following sentence, imagining that you are completely ecstatic and giddy with happiness:

"I'm going on vacation in two days."

Now, repeat the sentence above, but this time imagining that you were extremely unhappy, miserable, and sad. Observe the difference in the way that you sound. Practice with several sentences and alter the emotions you feel when you utter these sentences out loud. Practice with sentences while imagining that you feel impatient, angry, professional, business-like, disinterested, fatigued, and any other emotion you can think of. Imagine the emotion, then say the sentence out loud while pouring as much emotion into your delivery as you can.

Exercise #2

Pick a passage from a book, magazine, newspaper, or any online content. Each day spend at least 15-30 minutes (or any amount of spare time you have) reading these passages aloud.

As you do, once again imagine reading the sentence as though you were actually going through the emotions that the writer conveys. Include some facial expressions with your delivery if it helps. Don't hold back - you are practicing on your own with no one to impress. Be as over the top or as dramatic as you wish in your reading. The point is to pack as much feeling into what you are saying as possible, varying the tone of your voice.

A good tip would be to record yourself during these sessions, playing it back and see how you sound. Can you tell the emotions that you are supposed to feel based on the way you sound? If you can clearly distinguish one emotion from the next, you are doing a good job.

Exercise #3

This one works best if you have children at home, as you'll have plenty of access to children's books. Children's books are among the best practice material for vocal variation available. When you read aloud to a child, you tend to put a lot of variety into it, mixing up your voices based on the different characters in the book, and exaggerating your facial expressions for the entertainment of the child.

If you do have kids at home, go ahead, and use the time you spend reading to them as a way of practicing your vocal exercises. And if you do not have kids at home, you can still practice anyway with plenty of online resources that give you access to children's content through a quick Google search.

Banish the Monotony Once and for All

There are several benefits to be gained by getting rid of the monotony in your delivery, aside from the fact that your speeches and presentations improve by a mile. As your vocal variety improves:

- Your audience appreciates and respects you more as a speaker because they can see you are putting your heart into it.

- You become more interesting as a speaker, and your audience automatically becomes more interested in you.

- Your audience's interest is piqued, making them more receptive to the points that you are trying to make.

And of course, you are no longer seen as just any boring, forgetful speaker.

How Pitch Conveys Different Emotions and Messages

The ability to communicate well with the people around you is one of the most important life skills you can develop. Successful communication requires that you get your message across clearly and without a doubt. A great resource for emotionally powerful speeches is TED Talks, and one example of such a powerful performance is by speaker Hugh Herr. His speeches are a beautiful example of just how much emotions can go in terms of transcending the delivered content. THAT is the key to giving a great speech, captivating and engaging your audience right from the beginning.

Commonly referred to as "the art of persuasion," it takes great skill to convince others to see things the way that you want them to. When speaking, the goal is not to force others to accept your ideas, the goal is to use your skills to persuade and convince them to agree. To effectively do this, you need to tap into their emotions. It is often the way that you make someone *feel* that leaves the strongest impression. They may forget what you have said, but they will never forget the way you made them feel. If you have ever had fantastic customer experience where the staff member went above and beyond to make you feel valued, you'll know just how valuable a great experience can be. You can't recall just what the staff member might have said, but you do know they made you feel great, and the experience was top-notch from start to finish. You tell everyone that you meet what a great experience you had, too.

The right *emotional* delivery of your speech can recreate the same situation. Even if your audience can't recall word for word what you said during your presentation, they will still go out and spread the word to everyone they know about what a fantastic time they had. To create that memorable emotional encounter for your audience, you need to rely on using the right pitch to do it. Most public speakers tend just to do the easy thing and deliver the content they are supposed to. But that content will never reach the audience on an emotional level if your tone is not combined with the right pitch.

These two elements must work together to formulate the perfect delivery.

Your pitch, which is the high and low notes that you hit when you are speaking, should sound natural and pleasant. If your voice is far too high-pitched, you run the risk of being perceived as annoying or far too "squeaky" to your audience. That's not a sound they want to listen to for long! Having a pitch that is too low is not such a good thing either. Lower pitches are often associated with a sense of authority; you may come off sounding too bossy or commandeering – not something which is going to be well-received.

Many people do not realize that they aren't varying their vocal tone when speaking. Again, recording yourself is a great way to tell whether enough variation is taking place when you are speaking naturally. When listening, do you like the sound of your own voice? Chances are if you do not, your audience might not like it either; something needs to change if you are going to become the great public speaker that you want to be. That "something" is your pitch.

Creating the perfect emotional, pleasant experience for your audience means strengthening your message by varying to pitch of your voice based on what you are saying. When you ask a question, for example, end it with a higher pitch sound. When you make a statement, emphasize your point using lower pitches and tones.

Practicing Your Pitch Variety in Your Delivery

Before you begin any of these exercises, it is important that you record yourself during your practice sessions. Before you can begin refining your vocals for better public speaking sessions, you need first to *realize how you sound* to your audience. Recording yourself is the most accurate method of assessing your current vocal abilities, where your strengths and weaknesses lie. The way that you hear yourself is *not the same way others hear you.* Your voice is traveling through the bones in your head, and when that sound finally arrives at your ears, it sounds different to you than to others.

This is why how *we think we sound* is not actually how we sound to others.

An Exercise in Pitch

The best way to practice varying your pitch is through several read-aloud sessions. Just like exercises above to vary your tone, once again, you want to pick out several passages to read aloud, but this time, you are going to focus on reading these sentences with a different pitch.

Exercise #1

Pick one pitch to start with. It can be either high or low—it is up to you. Now, read your chosen passage aloud, maintaining the same pitch throughout until you reach the end. If you are starting off with the higher pitch, be sure to keep it high-pitched all throughout your reading. Once you are finished, switch your pitch! If you started with a higher pitch, you'd now be reading that same passage using the lower pitch instead.

Observe the effect that it has on you and how you feel when you use a higher and lower pitch. You should feel both an emotional and a physical difference.

Exercise #2

Once again, pick a passage. This time switch back and forth between your high and low pitch as you read aloud. Imagine your voice on a seesaw, alternating back and forth between the two pitches. You could start by reading the first sentence aloud in a high-pitched voice, and then switch to the lower pitch when you come to the second sentence. In the third sentence, switch to high pitch again, and back to low-pitched on the fourth sentence. Keep this going until you reach the end of your passage.

Once you have got comfortable with this, increase the difficulty level by switching pitches after every three words instead of between sentences. Read the first three words in a high-pitched voice, and then read the next three words using your lower tones. You can vary your pitch alterations as you like and play around with it.

Chapter 5: What's Happening with Your Hands?

Not everyone is going to feel comfortable standing in front of a crowd when they know several pairs of eyes are watching their every move. Being under the spotlight can make it hard to concentrate on what you should say, let alone remembering your breathing and body language at the same time. As if that is not enough, now you need to concentrate on what your hands are doing during your presentation! Yes, the hand signals you are unconsciously demonstrating could be sending out all the wrong signals without you even realizing it, yet it is another common mistake for new public speakers.

Your Gestures Matter

Remember how body language is 55% of the overall communication process? That includes your hand gestures, the subtle cues and signals that you give your audience - often without giving it too much thought. When was the last time you paid attention to what your hands were doing when you were speaking to someone – not while presenting or giving a speech, but just in everyday conversation with a friend or colleague? Do you think about what your hands are saying? Probably not, but the story that your hands tell could unwittingly be contributing to your message in a good (or bad) way.

Your Hand Signals Are Surprisingly Powerful

Research conducted on TED Talks revealed, not surprisingly, that the most popular and well-liked speakers were the ones who used twice as many hand gestures during their presentation. It wasn't just their fluctuating vocal tones and voice pitches that had audiences captivated—it was the various hand signals that they used to keep audiences tuned into the points they were making.

Nervous speakers who are uncomfortable being in front of a crowd need to rehearse their speeches with the accompanying hand gestures well beforehand. It's not going to work if you decide to "wing it" on that day. These influential speakers are so good at what they do *because* they've had plenty of experience and numerous practice hours clocked in before they reached their current level of competence.

Here's why the right-hand gestures can either make or break your message:

- With the right-hand gestures, you present yourself as a confident, composed public speaker who commands the room. Audiences respect that.

- Hand gestures can act as visual cues for your audience, helping to strengthen and further emphasize your points.

- Hand gestures are can be likened to those of an orchestra maestro. Your speech is the musical masterpiece that you are presenting while your gestures are the movements that tie it all together. Combined, they help audiences better focus on and appreciate what's being presented.

- Proper hand gesturing conveys that you are enthusiastic and passionate about what you are presenting (as opposed to standing on the stage stiff and barely making any movements). When we're excited, we naturally become more animated, and we gesture to emphasize that excitement. The same thing happens during a presentation.

• Your hands can help you better explain a point that you are trying to make. When you are trying to emphasize that the results of a study's findings are "smaller" than expected, using the accompanying hand gestures will help cement this fact into your audience's mind.

• Hand gestures make you appear more trustworthy. Inherently, humans are visual creatures, and we do not rely on words alone to be convinced by what someone is telling us. Which speaker would you trust the most? A speaker who gestures for emphasis or a speaker who has their hands in their pockets or stiffly by their sides the entire time?

• Your hand gestures mimic the thoughts that are going through your mind. Your words may sound confident and assured, but if your hand gestures do not match up to it, your audience will spot that immediately.

If you were to observe some of the most influential, memorable speakers and the way that they present themselves when addressing crowds, you'd notice that hand gestures are used to strengthen certain key aspects of their message. These influential speakers use *more* hand gestures than the average speakers do, and the gestures that they use are well-timed and crowd sensitive.

They know that the audience is paying attention to everything that they do, and they purposely use their body language for stressing particular points the *want the crowd to remember* most.

Using Correct Hand Gestures

Here's a fun fact about hand gestures: we were *all born to do it*! Researchers found that 18-month old toddlers who relied more on hand gestures to communicate went on to have greater language abilities as they got older. Hand gestures are a natural part of who we are as human beings.

Hand gestures are like a second language. Play a game of Charades, and it is obvious that our hands are tools capable of telling a story even in the absence of words. That does not mean, however, that you should gesture any which way you want when you are giving your presentation. No, the most effective public speakers are the ones who rely on a select, chosen few gestures that they learn to execute perfectly. Nervous public speakers suddenly become all too aware of their hands when they are in front of a crowd. Suddenly, hand gestures that normally flow when they are conversing with familiar people seem to disappear! When you are nervous, you forget what to do with your hands altogether, which explains why many new speakers stand stiffly in front of a crowd, looking awkward and extremely uncomfortable.

Sometimes new speakers swing to the other side, gesturing *far too much,* distracting their audience from the core message. Nervous speakers do not realize that they are hands are giving away how anxious they feel. Some examples of what nervous gesturing looks like include:

- "Wind-milling" hands, waving them all over the place
- Constantly pushing glasses back up onto the nose
- Playing with hair
- Clenching and unclenching the fists
- Wringing the hands
- Arms crossed in front of the body, tightly gripping the elbow of the opposite arm
- Thumping a podium or table too often to stress on a point
- Rubbing or scratching the nose too much
- Excessive finger-pointing directed towards the audience

To become an effective public speaker, you must become more aware of what your hands are doing. They need to enhance - not detract - from the message you are sending your audience. Unfortunately, most speakers won't be aware that their gesturing needs work unless someone points it out to them. A few simple rules to keep in mind when it comes to hand gestures are:

- Your hand gesture should clarify or supplement your points

- Your hand gestures should be natural, not obsessive

- Your hand gestures should be used mindfully and with intention

- Consider periodically clasping your hands together to prevent excessive gesturing

- Your palms should be displayed in an open manner, signaling honesty

Certain Hand Gestures Can Be Used to Make Your Speech More Effective and Engaging

If you want people to listen to you, you need to gesture with your hands. **Studies** have discovered that gestures make audiences take notice of your speech's acoustics. As these studies have revealed, hand gestures are not mere "add-ons" but exist for a specific purpose. Yes, hand gestures can be very powerful elements that contribute to your public speaking success. If you have ever been given advice along the way that tells you *not to use your hands too when giving a speech, toss* that advice out the window! The absence of gestures is not the answer to an effective speech. Hand gestures are still a necessity, but the key is to let the correct hand gestures do some of the talking.

The same TED Talks **research** mentioned above also discovered that the speeches which were the least popular were the ones that had an average of only 272 hand gestures incorporated into the presentation. The most popular ones (averaging 7.4 million viewers) had 465 hand gestures included in the speech that ran for the same amount of time as the least popular speeches. A typical struggle-point for speakers is deciding *what the correct hand gestures are* to help reinforce their messages - doing this while also remembering their speaking points. There's a lot that goes into trying to make a speech effective!

Hence, which hand gestures are considered effective and which are nothing more than a mere distraction? What should you use during your presentations to add power to your points? When in doubt, it is best to start with the following gestures:

- **Descriptive Gestures** - These gestures need to be pre-planned when you are practicing your speech. You may be tempted to gesture naturally on that day, but the danger with that approach us you could risk going overboard. Pre-planned, descriptive hand gestures can be a big help in your speeches. Descriptive gestures are used to help the audience stay in sync with what you are saying. If you are trying to make a small point, pinch or bring your fingers as close together as possible. If you are trying to illustrate a big point, expand your arms outwards to highlight what you are saying. When you are talking about numbers that range between one to 10, go ahead and show those numbers with your hands. These descriptive gestures help to paint a visual picture of your points within you audience's mind, helping them better remember your speech.

- **Open Your Palms** - Keeping your palms open is a common piece of advice related to body language. Subconsciously, people associate the open palm gesture as a sign that you have nothing to hide. When criminals are arrested, they are instructed to come out with their hands up as proof they have nothing to hide. Keeping your palms open and displayed to the audience encourages that element of trust because subliminally you are telling them you are exposed and there is nothing dishonest about your intentions.

- **Gesture Within the "Strike Zone"** - The "Strike Zone" is the area which spanning from your shoulders to the upper portion of your hips. Within this range is where your hand gestures appear the most natural, and ideally, you want to keep your gestures within this zone. Anything more than this and you risk gesturing in a distracting manner, rather than the effective one you are aiming for. Although it is not a hard and fast rule, it does err on the side of caution. It's okay if you need to gesture outside this zone occasionally.

- **The "Hand Over Heart" Gesture** - This is a good gesture to use when you are trying to emphasize that a certain point is particularly important to you. For example, when you are telling your audience during your speech that *"this cause is so important/matters a lot to me,"* placing your hand over your heart as the accompanying gesture adds that emotional element to your words.

- **The Double Hand Gesture** - Use this only when you need to use your hands to represent two groups or two important points that you want to draw the audience's attention to. Using both hands to gesture as you speak is useful when you are comparing two opposing points. This makes it easier for your audience to keep track of the two points that you are referring to. When you talk about Point A, for example, raise your left hand to remind your audience that Point A is what they should be focusing on right now. When you talk about Point B, raise your right hand and lower the left. This reminds the crowd that a different point of view is being addressed now, and their focus should now be shifted to Point B. The double hand gesture is useful in situations where you need to help your audience keep track of what's going on so that they aren't left behind each time you switch tracks.

Hand Gesturing Mistakes to Avoid

It was briefly touched on above what some examples of nervous hand gesturing look like. Remember the mannerisms we discussed in Chapter Two? Hand gestures fall into this category of nervous mannerisms that come out when you find yourself in a less than comfortable situation (like being in the spotlight and having to make a speech in front of everyone!) Playing with your hair, fiddling with objects in your hand, tugging at your clothes, picking at your nails, putting your hands in your pockets, flailing your arms in an uncoordinated manner are all examples of what *not to do* when you are giving a speech.

If in doubt and you are *still* not sure what to do with your hands when you are presenting, here are a couple of fallback gestures you can turn to:

- **Using Your Full Hand** - Pointing with your fingers at the slides or the audience is a less than desirable gesture. However, it is surprising just how many speakers make the mistake of inadvertently pointing to their presentation slides with their middle finger (yikes!) Pointing is never a recipe for success, especially if you are presenting in a foreign country where the gestures may signal something else. The worst thing you could do as a speaker is to give off a rude gesture and not even realize it. If you do need to point, the safest thing would be to use your whole hand instead.

- **No Fingers Near the Face** - The use of fingers can sometimes have unintended negative consequences. If you keep running your fingers through your hair, using it to push your glasses up repeatedly, scratch or rub your nose, or really touch any part of your face or body repeatedly, your audience is not going to be concentrating on what you are saying. They're going to be focused instead on your physical appearance. They'll automatically stop listening to you and start getting curious about why you are repeatedly doing this—which is why it is important to practice your speech several times before you give it, recording it if possible. You may have bad mannerisms or habits that you are not even aware of! Should you observe any of these mannerisms, make a note of this and assign specific hand gestures to accompany parts of your speech. This way, your fingers do not have the freedom to do as they please.

- **Avoid Your Fingernails** - Treat your fingernails as a taboo area during your speech. Don't touch them, do not play with them, do not even think about them at all if you can help it. A nervous tick that many speakers tend to be guilty of is playing or picking at their fingernails when they are speaking. To you, it may not mean anything because you do not realize what you are doing. But to your audience who's watching your every move, it means something else entirely. Picking at your fingernails gives the impression that you are bored, your mind is somewhere else, and you are not fully present in the moment. Just like the finger rule above, when you aren't sure what to do with your hands, assign specific, strong hand gestures to each portion of your presentation, practicing until you get it right. You need to do something with your hands to keep them from doing the wrong thing. Read the portions of your speech that do not have any specific gestures at the moment, making note of which gestures you believe would be most beneficial to include in your speech.

- **No Wedding Ring Fiddling** - Nervous speakers are guilty of this if they wear a wedding ring. This often happens during the "awkward" phase of the presentation, when the talk is over, and you are standing there on the stage - sometimes in silence - as you wait for the audience to ask any questions they might have. As they glance out at their audience to see who has questions, these speakers will subconsciously be twisting or playing with their wedding rings. This speaks volumes to your audience. Either the speaker is nervous, or the speaker is impatient, ready to exit and call it a day! The wedding-ring-twist does not look professional, and even if you have done everything right up to that point, your entire presentation could be killed just by that one gesture alone. To keep yourself from doing this, steeple your fingers together as you patiently wait for some questions to come in.

- **Stay Away from the "Clinton Thumb"** - You'll notice a lot of politicians making this mistake. The Clinton Thumb involves your thumb resting on top of your fist. Doing this makes you look aggressive to your audience, especially if you pound the podium or the table when you do. Bill Clinton and John F. Kennedy may have done it, but that is not a good gesture to include in your public speaking sessions. It simply does not look natural. Choose to either steeple your hands together or drop them down to your sides for a minute or two (but not in a stiff manner) as you move on to your next point and prepare the next set of gestures for your speech. Keeping your hands by your sides is a quick reset button for when no hand gestures seem to feel right. Just remember not to leave them there for too long.

- **Stay Away from the Groin** - You would be surprised at just how many speakers make the mistake of clasping their hands in front of the groin area. That is absolutely the *wrong* move to make because it is only drawing your audience's attention to all the wrong places. This does not just apply to men either; women can be just as guilty of making this mistake. Clasping them in this way is not an effective use of your hand gestures and it may make you look awkward and uncomfortable. When in doubt, always use the hand steeple as your fallback move, and quickly move onto some other hand gesture for the rest of your speech.

- **Avoid Holding on to Objects** - Holding onto objects in your hand during your speech is risky because you might end up fiddling with them the entire time. Although experienced public speakers do hold pointers to help them transition from one slide to the next, they are conscious of what their hands are doing. You'll rarely ever see them fiddling with anything in their hands, as they do not want to distract their audience from the key message. If you do need to hold onto a pointer for your slides, be so subtle and discreet about it that your audience does not even know there is something in your hands.

•

Chapter 6: The Language of the Eyes

Pay close attention to the eyes; they may reveal that there is more to the story than what you are being told. When a person avoids eye contact, there is a strong possibility that they are uncomfortable, disinterested, nervous, bored, or all the above. If their pupils are dilated, it is safe to say that they are comfortable, perhaps they like you. If they are blinking far too much (in an unnatural way), there is a strong possibility that they may not be entirely honest with you. If they often look to the left, they could be recalling a genuine memory. If they often look to the right, it could be a sign that they are trying to make something up. Body language can be fascinating, almost like you are a detective trying to unravel the different layers of the story and get to the bottom of the truth.

Eye Contact and Public Speaking

As you can probably tell by now, there are a lot of factors contributing to your success as an effective public speaker, including your overall posture, breathing, the way that you carry yourself, the way you stand, and hand gestures. Another element to learn is *your eye contact.* If there was one thing you could do to enhance your presentation and the impact that you have as a speaker, it would be maintaining purposeful, deep eye contact with the members of your audience. Of course, it is impossible to do this with everyone, especially those seated all the way at the back of the room, too distant to see. However, for the audience members that you *can* connect wit - the ones seated in the first few rows at the front - that is what you should be doing.

There was an interesting experiment that researchers at Cornell University carried out. In a **study** published in the *Environment and Behavior* journal, the researchers took the cartoon rabbit on the Trix™ cereal boxes and manipulated its gaze. As a result of that one manipulation of the rabbit is eyes, adults were more likely to choose Trix™ over other cereal brands if the rabbit looked directly at them instead of looking away. Eye contact, as the researchers of this experiment discovered, invoked powerful emotions and feelings within the customer, and that sense of connection was what made them more likely to buy this cereal. Even a cartoon rabbit is eye contact makes a difference!

If you want to connect to your audience, you *must* look into their eyes as much as possible during your presentation. It's easier to do this when you are presenting in a meeting room full of colleagues at work; the room is likely smaller, with less listeners. In a larger venue, maintaining good eye contact with every audience member is a bit more challenging.

It's going to be to your advantage as a speaker, though, to lock eyes with your audience when you are addressing them, no matter the size of the crowd. Here's what good eye contact can do for you as a speaker:

- It allows you to appear more authoritative as a speaker, making you appear more believable in the eyes of your audience. Someone who knows what they are talking about will have no problems looking others in the eye and telling them the facts.

- It helps you concentrate on who you are targeting. Allowing your eyes to wander aimlessly could lead to distractions as you take in the external images or stimuli that are happening around the room.

- When you look them in the eye, your listener beings to focus on you instead of being distracted by their thoughts. It's hard not to pay attention when someone is looking you straight in the eye, and if you want to get your audience to focus, this is one way to do it.

- When your audience focuses on returning your eye contact, there is a greater chance that they are listening to what you are telling them. You are increasing the odds of your message resonating with your listeners.

- It helps to transform your audience from passive to active participants. When you look them in the eye, you are creating a connection, and it makes them feel as though you are speaking directly to them. Suddenly, your speech is no longer a speech, but a personal conversation which they are keen to participate in. Eye contact will help them keep up with your message.

- It gives you the opportunity to spot when your audience might need more convincing. When you make eye contact with them, you are simultaneously reading their facial expressions. When you see skepticism in their face, it gives you the chance to step in and convince them before moving onto your next point. Acknowledging their concerns by saying, *"I know it seems difficult to believe, but here's why it makes sense,"* will change the way that your speech is being received. Audiences will be intrigued when you appear to be able to answer their unspoken thoughts and convince them without them having to ask for more details. That's the power of good eye contact.

- It will force you to naturally slow down as you speak when you are looking someone in the eye anywhere from 3–5 seconds. Former President Barack Obama employed this tactic to help him become a more powerful orator.

- It allows you to be both empathetic and assertive at the same time. You can share your opinion with your listeners, and at the same time observe their reaction, better understanding how they are responding to your message.

Good eye contact with your audience makes them feel like they matter. Despite being part of a large crowd, they get to feel involved in your presentation almost like it was tailor-made for them. In turn, you appear more approachable and a silent rapport is formed between you and the audience as you continue to engage them in your presentation with your eyes.

Strong Posture Makes a Difference

With the seemingly long list of things to do and remember for an effective presentation, it is easy to forget that your posture has to remain perfect through it all. If you are going to try and breathe the right way and give as much power to your vocals as possible, you are going to need good posture to support you through that effort. Proper posture does not just give the appearance of being someone who is confident and assured—it is also necessary to ensure that you are not breathing through your chest throughout your speech.

In Chapter 1, we discussed how being one with your breath is one of the most important techniques you need to master to become a masterful public speaker. Since the power of breath is so important, the subject is broached here once again, this time focusing on how it is linked to your posture. There's a lot of advice out there when it comes to public speaking, but the one piece to remember is:

breathing through your chest is never going to be good for your posture when you are presenting.

Breathing through your chest is poor practice because:

- It facilitates a lot of tension in your upper body. When you are tense, it is going to negatively impact your posture, which eventually affects your public speaking capabilities.

- Chest breaths can't give you the same kind of sound quality that deep breathing can. When you are taking shorter breaths, you compromise your pitch, tone, volume, resonance, and overall sound quality of your voice. Only deep breathing promotes good posture.

- You're not fully utilizing your natural breathing mechanism when you breathe through your chest. By taking shorter breaths, you are not encouraging the use of your abdominal and diaphragm area, which are also an essential part of your breathing process.

When you are nervous, taking shorter and sharper breathes only makes it more apparent! You will appear panicked when your breathing is visibly quick and rapid, heaving and panting. Also, it is impossible to maintain good posture when you are not engaging your abdominal region. Think of your body as if it were a pipe. What happens when the pipe has bends or curves instead of being straight? It produces blockages. Those bends and blockages affect the flow of air through those pipes. It's the same thing with your body. If you were presenting behind a podium or a desk, any kind of bend forward or slump is going to make it hard for you to breathe properly; the quality of your voice *will be* compromised. The advice to hold your head up and stand up tall is not just for the benefit of the audience, but for *your breathing* benefit, too.

You probably understand by now: maintaining good posture is essential if you want your presentation to be considered a success.

Not only does it make you appear confident, it also provides the following benefits:

- Taking deep breaths when your posture is correct helps feel calmer and more in control of your emotions.

- When you look authoritative, audiences tend to pay more attention to you compared to a speaker who looks visibly nervous, hunched, or appears as though they wish the ground would swallow them up!

- Good posture makes it easy for you to speak with clarity, so your words ring loud and clear across the entire room.

- It helps to create a better first impression among your audience. When you walk onto that stage with a strong, tall posture, the immediate first impression given is resoundingly positive. Now, imagine you were in the audience, watching a speaker enter the stage shuffling their feet, looking awkward with their shoulders rolled forward almost as if they were trying to retreat into themselves. Which speaker would leave a better impression in your mind?

- A strong posture conveys enthusiasm, and when you are excited about what you should say, your audience will sense that. Listeners are affected by your emotions – they can't help but feel what you feel.

Tips on Improving Your Posture

Ideally, you'd want to practice maintaining good posture every day and throughout the day, but that is not always possible. It's easy to forget about posture as you get caught up in your daily tasks. When you do remember, though, it is easy enough to work on improving your posture and to do it so subtly that no one even realizes you are doing it.

To improve your posture, straighten your back, imagining that there is a string at the top of your head that is pulling and lengthening your entire body upwards. When you are straightened as tall as you can, roll your shoulders back, tilt your chin forward slightly and lift your head up high. If there are people around you, try to imagine yourself attempting to peer over the tops of everyone's head. You should do this quick little exercise on the go or at home whenever you remember to be mindful of your posture. You should *especially* do it before your presentation. The more you exercise, the easier it will be to maintain good posture for longer periods until it eventually becomes second nature.

To help you maintain good posture, stand like this when facing a crowd:

- Your weight should be mostly on the balls of your feet, not on your toes, and evenly distributed across both feet.

- In order to avoid unnaturally standing ramrod straight, keep your knees slightly bent as you continue to lengthen through your spine.

- Stand with your feet no more than shoulder-width apart.

- As you stand tall and roll your shoulders back, tuck your stomach in for better balance.

- Keep your head level at all times. A good reminder is to check if your earlobes and your shoulders are in line. Your head should not be too far forward or too far back. Keep it in a nice, even line with your shoulder.

Tips to Improve Your Eye Contact

Instead of seeing your audience as a large group, start to think of them as one listener. From the moment you walk on stage and greet the crowd, start scanning the room and look around for friendly, warm, and welcoming faces. That's your first step to building a connection with them, shifting your gaze from one audience member to another as you hold each gaze for three to five seconds at a time. Once you have established that initial connection, these are some other things you can do to improve that visual connection with your listeners:

- **Focus on Everyone** - This one is much easier to do when you present to a smaller crowd, such as in a meeting room at your workplace. In a larger crowd, aim to connect with as many members of the audience as you can. An easy way to do this is to divide your audience into different segments or groups, and then choose several members of the group to make eye contact with.

- **Connect Just Long Enough to Make a *Connection*** - You do not have to hold their gaze for too long or make eye contact with only the same few audience members. That's going to be impractical, as you are only allocated a certain period of time for your speech. What you need to aim for instead, is to make eye contact long enough for you to establish some sort of connection with them. During a presentation, each eye contact session should last no more than five seconds, which is the average time it takes to finish a train of thought. This way, you do not risk losing track of what you are saying, and the five-second rule encourages you to slow down the rate of your speech.

- **Avert When Sensing Discomfort** - Bear in mind that not everyone in your audience is going to be comfortable with direct eye contact. Some participants are shy individuals, preferring to blend into the crowd instead of feeling like they've been singled out. You need to be able to scan their emotions quickly when you are making eye contact—and as soon as you sense them feeling uncomfortable (shifting their eyes or fidgeting slightly in their seats), avert your gaze and move onto the next audience member. This is an important tip to keep in mind when you are presenting or speaking in a foreign country, as some cultures consider it offensive to make eye contact.

- **Connect During the Critical Parts** - There will be some points you wish to drill into the minds of listeners; time these key points so they match with eye contact you make. When it is time to emphasize a point, make sure you are holding the gaze of an audience member and look right at them as you get the point across. Your ability to combine eye contact with emotion will make your presentation much stronger.

- **Meet Your Audience Beforehand** – Whenever possible, try to meet at least a few audience members before you take the stage. When you walk in, you already have a few friendly faces to engage with! It can be difficult to make an immediate connection with total strangers, so it to introduce yourself to your audience beforehand, learning as few names as possible. Allowing listeners to get to know you personally *prior to your presentation* makes they feel engaged when you connect with them again on that stage.

- **Watch for the Nod** - During your speech, one important audience reaction to watch for is "the nod." When your audience member feels like you have been talking to them and is feeling engaged and connected, they will subconsciously let you know by nodding along with what you are saying. When a person understands and processes what you have just said, they will nod to signal that, and you can take that as your cue that your message has been well received. It's also a great tip to pace yourself when you are speaking, by waiting for your audience to nod and signal that they've understood before moving on to your next point.

- **Avoid the "Lighthouse" Connection** - The "lighthouse" connection here is when a speaker moves around the room so quickly that it is impossible to make any real contact long enough to leave an impression. Like the light shining from a lighthouse, moving and scanning the ocean so quickly and systematically that it is already made a loop around and come back again before you can count to five. If you are scanning the room in this rapid, systematic manner, you are failing to make any real connections with your audience.

- **Don't Linger with Long Sentences -** You need to know when to move on, even if you are in the middle of a long sentence when you do. If you try maintaining eye contact with one audience member per sentence (exceeding the five-second), you run the risk of making that person feel uncomfortable. Your audience wants to feel connected, not *targeted.* If you do need to make the shift during a long sentence, make it subtle and gradually shift your gaze to the person sitting next to a time. Make it natural, not abrupt.

Quick Bonus Tip

When you are giving a speech across cultures, it helps to do some research, taking note of your listener's cultural norms. Showing sensitivity and respect for another culture's beliefs and perspective shows your empathy as a speaker, and your audience will look upon you favorably for demonstrating that kind of consideration.

In some Asian cultures, it is considered disrespectful to make eye contact, especially if you happen to be a subordinate. In Middle Eastern cultures, it is thought to be inappropriate for members of the opposite sex to make eye contact as it might denote romantic interests.

Chapter 7: Getting Over the Stage Fright Hump

What if you were told that even some of the best performers or public speakers out there had, at one time or another, experienced stage fright, too? Barbra Streisand, Meryl Streep, Elvis, Sir Laurence Olivier – all have admitted that they have had their fair share of stage fright jitters. It's perfectly normal to feel worried, anxious, and maybe even afraid at the thought of standing in front of a crowd and communicating in public. Not everyone was born with a natural love for the spotlight, and most exceptional public speakers today had to get over their own feelings of anxiety in terms of speaking in public. If they could overcome it, you certainly can, too.

More than 80% of the population experiences some form of anxiety or stage fright when asked to perform or present in public. Some might be reluctant to admit it, for fear of being perceived as weak, especially in a work environment where there is a lot of pressure to deliver exceptional performance for the sake of the job. However, denying the way that you feel is not going to help you in that department, either. Acknowledging your fears and gaining understanding of why you feel that way is the first step towards overcoming the stage fright hump once and for all.

Understanding What Stage Fright Is

Another term that is often used to refer to stage fright is *performance anxiety*. Typically, these emotions are experienced before you must make a public speech, perform or present for an audience. In some cases, stage fright can also be experienced when you know you must perform in front of a camera. Stage fright occurs in four stages:

- *The Anticipation* - Before the actual performance or public speaking session, the anticipation of what's to come can send your nerves into a tailspin. We tend to anticipate the worst, running all sorts of possible scenarios through our mind concerning what could go wrong on the day. These negative emotions contribute to the performance anxiety that we might be feeling.

- *The Avoidance* - Out of sheer nervousness, many might think about avoiding having to perform at all. Knowing there is no way out of the presentation can increase feelings of anxiety before the event.

- *The Panic* - This tends to occur right before you are expected to perform. It is not uncommon for many to experience sheer panic moments before taking the stage.

- *The Appraisal* - Performance anxiety can also take place *after* your big speech or performance. Some performers, upon reflection of how they think they did after the event, occasionally experience mild stage fright just recollecting the experience. This might put them off ever wanting to perform in public again.

Why Do We Experience Stage Fright?

There could be several reasons behind this, depending on your personality and past experiences. The most common reason is a lack of self-confidence. When speakers or performers do not believe in themselves enough, this leads to feelings of inadequacy.

Other possible reasons include a lack of preparation, fear of embarrassing or humiliating themselves in public; some performers even experience anxiety when they believe the audience is going to criticize them behind their backs.

Stage fright is physiological. When your body is faced with a stimulus, your immediate reaction can be either one of two things: feelings of excitement or feelings of fear. In the case of performing in public, it is often the latter that gets triggered, as very rarely does anyone feel immediate excitement when being told that they must perform in front of an audience. This stimulus triggers the adrenalin in your body—a hormone secreted to help you cope with the stimulus. Adrenalin, in turn, triggers the *fight or flight response*, which sometimes manifests into physical symptoms like shaking, difficulty breathing, rapid heartbeat, trembling, and even stomachache. These symptoms indicate that you are experiencing stage fright.

Are There Any Other Stage Fright Symptoms?

There could be several ways in which a person might respond to stage fright. This would depend on the level of anxiety they feel, as well as how badly they are affected by it. Stage fright symptoms are classified into two categories, emotional and physical.

Some of the common physical symptoms one might experience with stage fright include:

- Cold, shaking hands
- Rapid heartbeat
- Dry mouth
- Nausea
- Nervous mannerisms
- Visible trembling or shaking
- Weak in the knees

- Nausea

- Nervous flutters in the stomach

- Flushed or red face

Emotional symptoms associated with stage fright include:

- Feeling like your thoughts are racing all over the place

- Feelings of inadequacy or incompetence, which lead to emotional upset

- Anxiety about messing up what you need to say

- Fear of being embarrassed when you on the stage

- Feeling claustrophobic as if the room is closing in, struggling to remain calm or to breathe properly

In severe cases of stage fright, it is not uncommon for the speaker or performer to freeze on stage, unable to speak at all.

Is It Possible to Overcome Stage Fright?

Absolutely! With the right coping techniques, overcoming stage fright is entirely possible. The following measures are recommended for those seeking to deal with their nervous jitters and control their emotions before they take the stage:

- **Relaxation Exercises** - Meditation and yoga are among the recommended exercises to help cope with performance anxiety. Relaxation techniques are an effective way of alleviating the symptoms associated with the stress that the body feels when plagued by the emotional roller-coaster triggered by having to perform or present in public. If you need physical assistance to help alleviate your stress, *Shiatsu* massages (an Oriental massage technique) focuses on the pressure points of the body, working to relieve stress from those targeted areas.

- **Physical Exercises** - Relaxation exercises help to de-stress the mind, and physical exercises help you channel your anxious emotions externally in a healthy manner. Stage fright can cause a lot of negative, unhealthy emotions within you, and keeping them pent up is not an effective coping mechanism. You need to get the stress that you feel out of your body, and one approach to that is through physical exercise. For example, running, aerobics, kickboxing, hiking, and Zumba are exercises which not only help you work up a good sweat session, but they promote the release of endorphins in your body. Endorphins are brain chemicals that help you feel happier and calmer—which is just what you need to deal with stage fright. There's also a quick little exercise that you can do right before you take the stage: rub your hands together as fast as you can, focusing on releasing all your anxiety through the motion. Another easy exercise is shaking your hands as fast as you can, putting all your energy into it at your fastest speed possible. Picture yourself shaking away the anxiety from your body.

- **Watching Your Diet** - The food you eat could be affecting your anxiety levels. If you are already feeling particularly nervous, avoid caffeinated beverages like tea and coffee right before your presentation. Caffeine is a known stimulant for jitters, and you certainly do not need the extra push; you are probably already nervous enough as it is! The best beverage to consume is water, making sure to stay well hydrated before and during your presentation to prevent the dry mouth sensation.

Understanding Speech Anxiety

Anxiety has a way of affecting our bodies in the most unpleasant way. No one likes feeling anxious, and we certainly do not want others to know just how jumbled our emotions are on the inside.

Not everyone is going to experience extreme stage fright, but most people will feel some level of speech anxiety when they must address a large group of people. Some people claim that public speaking is their greatest fear. Very rarely that you are going to find anyone who can confidently tell you they feel absolutely no fear at all when they have to present in front of an audience—so rare, in fact, that finding this one person is going to be like trying to find a needle in a haystack.

Don't be fooled by the calm, confident composure that you see many of today's renowned public speakers as they present. They are not completely worry-free;

they have simply learned how to control and handle their performance anxieties, turning that into a strength used to boost their performance. On the inside, they could be feeling just as nervous as you are! Although you may be trembling and shaking like a leaf on the inside, most of the time the sheer extent of your anxiety is not immediately visible to the audience. If you do a good job of covering it up, most people won't be able to tell that you are feeling nervous at all. Take comfort in the fact that your anxiety can remain hidden from the audience if you play your cards right.

Speech anxiety is not as bad as it may initially seem. The most anxious moments tend to happen *before* the speech, as you have no idea how is going to go; your mind may be whirling with all the possible ways which you might mess up. Once you take the stage and progress through your speech, you will likely begin feeling less anxious as you get closer to the end. Right before the speech, your anxiety levels might be at the highest point, but it gradually starts to fade away once your speech is in motion. By the time you reach the end, most people find their anxiety levels have dissipated, and they start to feel much better.

Anxiety is an all too common condition these days. In fact, anxiety has become the most **common form of mental illness**, affecting approximately 18% of adults. So, if you are worried that you are at a disadvantage because you seem to be coping with speech anxiety where others seem normal, do not be. Speech anxiety - along with other forms of anxiety-like phobias and generalized anxiety disorders - are more common than you think. When someone tells you that they have "butterflies" in their stomach or that they feel like they may vomit before a speech or presentation, that is form of speech anxiety. They may not be having a full-blown panic attack over it, but speech anxiety can manifest itself in minor ways, too.

Our bodies respond to fear in a powerful way. The most common symptoms experienced with speech anxiety are often racing hearts, shallow and rapid breathing, and cortisol – the hormone responsible for triggering those stressful emotions that we feel. Other general symptoms associated with speech anxiety might include sweating, light-headedness, upset stomach, possible nausea, and a shaky, unsteady voice. It may not be possible to eliminate anxiety over your public speaking moments completely, but there are a few ways you could deal with it to minimize the impact that speech anxiety has on your mind and body. Fortunately, these simple techniques will help you deal with speech anxiety and provide some much-needed relief when you need it most:

- *Technique #1 - Progressive Relaxation.* Best done while you are at home, lie down comfortably on your back. Keep your arms and your legs uncrossed as you do. Now, visualize a warm, comforting feeling that starts at the top of your head. This is where you imagine releasing all the tension that you feel from your body. After several deep breaths, imagine that warm sensation slowly traveling down towards the rest of your body. As you exhale each breath, feel the tension leaving your body. You should feel lighter and lighter and more relaxed with each breath that you take.

- *Technique #2 - Avoid Negative Self-Talk.* Avoid any kind of talk that is even bordering on negativity. In fact, avoid bleakness and cynicism all together! Whenever you notice your mind circling around a gloomy thought, put a stop to it, immediately shifting your thoughts to something positive that is ahead for you. It is extremely helpful to have several positive mantras or inspirational sayings on hand to help you turn your thoughts around and squash down the negative ones that threaten to aggravate your anxiety levels.

- *Technique #3 - Focus on Your Top Qualities.* This is an exercise you can work on before your presentation. Pick three things about yourself that you like and what you believe are your strengths. If you are struggling with this, enlist the help of a friend or family member to help you pinpoint some of your best qualities. Once you have picked three qualities that you like, repeat these qualities in your head, focusing on feeling good about yourself each time you do it. Repeated this activity every day until you can mentally focus on these qualities – truly believing that you have them - and even with a smile on your face! This exercise helps reaffirm in your head and heart that you possess worthwhile and beneficial characteristics. Focus on your excellent attributes, feel the confidence, and believe that you are capable of handling this presentation.

- *Technique #4 - Identifying Your Triggers.* A big part of overcoming your speech anxiety includes being able to identify your triggers – getting to the root cause of what's making you feel so worried. Understanding the source of your fears will make it easier for you to break down those fears, allowing your mind to analyze and decide if there is a valid cause for concern. For example, once you have identified that your speech anxiety is stemming from the fear of what the audience might think about you, examine that trigger and identify if there is a *valid cause* for concern. Is there any evidence that you are going to be judged or criticized? Why do you believe your audience might think poorly of you? Have any past experiences given you a reason to believe that the audience might be judging you harshly? If they do think that way about you, are their thoughts going to impact your life in any significant way? As you slowly start to unravel the layers and find that your trigger is based on mostly assumptions, it is easier to keep yourself calm using logic and reason.

Don't forget about the deep breathing exercises and techniques that you learned in Chapter 1! In every exercise that you do to help you alleviate your anxieties over public speaking, always go back to *being one with your breath*. Deep, diaphragmatic breathing will get you through it.

Addressing the Negative Thoughts That Hold You Back

Anxiety and excessive worry are not feelings that should be taken lightly. Any kind of anxiety should be taken seriously; there have been instances where chronic worriers are so anxiety-ridden that they begin seeking out out harmful habits. Such habits (alcohol, drugs, smoking and even overeating) often represents an attempt to make themselves feel better, providing only temporary, short-term relief. These "answers" never work for long because they do not get to the root of the problem. Speech anxiety could border on these severe levels for some, and if you happen to be among those people who are deeply affected by this form of anxiety, do not dismiss it as something that is "just in your head."

In any area of your life where you hope to achieve success, there is one crucial element that must be present—*a positive attitude.* Unfortunately, it seems that more people today are plagued with negative emotions and thoughts more than ever before - possibly due to the very stressful lives most of us lead these days. The world may be a much easier place to live in, but it is also a complicated place. We have a lot more going on today than several decades ago, and the further we advance, the more reasons we seem to have to worry. We agonize about our lives, our future, our families, friends, job, kids - sometimes we even become overwrought about how to deal with those worries! Of course, we concern ourselves about giving speeches and embarrassing ourselves in public, too.

Negative thoughts prevent you from moving forward. When you are crippled by them, it becomes harder for you to focus on anything else, let alone progressing forward. Thus, is it imperative that you take the necessary steps to help you overcome these negative thoughts. They will only be a hindrance in your life *if you allow them to*, and this is what you need to do to put a stop to them once and for all:

- Stop comparing yourself to others—their story is not your story. You are living your own life, progressing at your own rate; trying to keep up with others when you are not ready is only going to leave you feeling frustrated and morally dejected.

- Stop overlooking your own accomplishments and start celebrating the victories you gain -even the little triumphs. Every step forward can server to reinforce your self-confidence, reminding you of the many things you are capable of. Treat yourself to a little self-praise!

- Stop second-guessing yourself—it will only cause you to spiral further down the negative slope. Be confident with the decisions you have made. Even if the outcomes seem like a mistake, be assured that there is a possible lesson to be learned from it, and that – in itself – is progress.

- Stop spending too much time with toxic individuals—they will only serve to feed into your negative thoughts and fears. Instead, surround yourself with like-minded people – those who have accomplished successes of their own, and those who inspire you to do better.

- Stop believing by default that everything is going to go badly. Unless you have proof that things are not going well, try working on the assumption that everything is going to perfectly. Turn that negative assumptions into positive beliefs!

- Stop judging yourself too harshly and learn to forgive yourself when you make mistakes. Mistakes are how we learn, and they are nothing to be ashamed of. They make us stronger, better, and wiser—which then leads to better decisions in the future.

Be Yourself. You are Good Enough

Putting a lot of expectations on ourselves to be someone that we're not only adds to the stress of speaking in public. You'd be surprised at just how much a big part of your public speaking worries comes from the pressure for perfection – a pressure that *you have placed on yourself.*

You *do not need* to be someone that you are not. You have plenty to offer by being yourself, and you do not have to pretend to be someone else. You do not have to be extremely charming, and you do not have to have the qualities of a movie star to be successful on stage. Being genuine and comfortable with who you are is often the best thing you can do for your performance, and when you embrace your own unique individuality, it takes a lot of pressure and weight off your shoulders.

Chapter 8: Push Without Being Pushy

Persuasion takes great skill. It's not easy to convince others to see things the way that you want them to. It's not impossible, but it takes a certain skill and ability to gently "push" them towards your point of view without being *pushy*. This technique is commonly referred to as *the art of persuasion*. You're *not forcing* them to go along with and accept the new ideas that you are presenting—you are simply channeling your communication skills *to persuade and convince* them to come around. Marketers and advertisers use this all the time—even salespeople sway customers into making a purchase from their business. Motivational speakers inspire change in others by persuading them to see the benefits of what great change can do for their lives. Steve Jobs, a man renowned for his ability to charm and persuade on stage, caused Apple's sales to soar after each presentation that he made.

Certainly, the art of persuasion is a valuable skill set to possess—but how do we learn to harness those powers of persuasion? Then, how do we then use those powers to our advantage during the speeches and presentations we give?

Persuading Your Audience in A Subtle Manner

The most effective speakers can convince their audiences and sway opinions without having to resort to being overly pushy, aggressive, or bulldozing their opinions unto others. Effective persuasion requires an entirely different approach. You need to take a step back and rely on empathy to understand where the other person might be coming from. Nobody likes being told they are wrong, and they especially do not like to feel as though they are being forced to change. They *definitely do not want* to have to sit through a presentation feeling as though ideas are being crammed down their throat against their will. Do that, and the only guaranteed outcome: you are going to lose your listener's attention, and their will to be attentive.

A subtler approach to persuasion is going to be far more effective. Arguing and debating the pros and cons with your audience will only take you so far. Demonstrating empathy, validating their emotions, *and then* working together with them to arrive at a happy and comfortable outcome: that is the very best way to persuade without being pushy.

The art of persuasion is called *an art* for a reason. It is not just about telling your audience what they should or shouldn't do. If you truly want to convince them through your presentation, you must make them believe in what you are telling them. They need to believe in it so much they are willing to take action; that is how the greatest speakers inspire change. You want your audience to leave your presentation with renewed motivation and eager to explore or further investigate the options you presented. You want them to leave your presentation, thinking, *"Wow! That was a fantastic speech!"*

To persuade without being pushy, you are going to have to be:

- **Trustworthy** - No one is going to be convinced by anything you say if they do not believe that they can trust you. You are a stranger to them in most cases, unless you are presenting to a room full of your colleagues or business associates. When you are not known to your listeners, they are not likely to trust you the minute you step out onto that stage. You wouldn't trust someone you do not know, so why would they? But if you are honest and transparent and display all the right body language signals (open palms and good eye contact), as you progress throughout your speech, it becomes easier to convince them once they start getting comfortable. Once they see you are honest enough, they will be a lot more willing to consider changing their point of view. If you are in a situation where you are pressed for time to build trust (like when you are giving a speech), try building your case instead based on credible or reputable sources that are known to be trustworthy. Incorporate these reputable sources into your presentation as an added element of credibility.

- **Attuned to Their Needs** - What matters the most to your audience? Why are they here listening to your speech? If you want your message to resonate with your crowd, you need to speak to them where it touches them the most. Touch on the emotional element that was discussed previously. When you connect with them on the issues that matter most and what's important to them, you'll have a much easier time persuading them to see things from the angle you are presenting.

- **Confident Enough to Guarantee** - Only guarantee something if you are absolutely sure of what you are saying. If you believe that your recommendations are *the best and only* approach to go with, go out on a limb and reassure your audience by offering some kind of guarantee that would make them feel better about changing their mind. A "guarantee" might look something like this: *"Believe me, this works, and I'm living proof of that!"* Only do this if you are sure there is no way this could backfire, or you might risk hurting your credibility.

- **Honest About the Good and Bad -** It's easier to subtly sway your audience into seeing things from your perspective if you are - once again - transparent about your arguments. Don't just talk about the positives in an attempt to persuade them. You need to present both sides of the story, the good and the bad, and then gently nudge them towards the side that you would like them to take. People are easier to convince when they believe that they arrived at the solution on their own. Use your gentle guidance to steer them in the right direction, and then let the final decision rest with them. Give them the opportunity to believe that arriving at a conclusion was due to their deductive reasoning; it was their idea all along!

- **Eager Without Sounding Desperate -** You may be eager to persuade them to change their minds but be careful not to let that eagerness show too much, or you might come across as desperate. Nothing pushes people away faster than desperation, and to avoid this, you need to take yourself out of the equation. Make your presentation all about *them, not you.*

- **Agreeable with Their Point of View -** During the Q&A portion of the presentation, you need to address and acknowledge their concerns, and even agree with their point of view as a display of empathy. Remember that no one likes to feel pressured into doing anything, and you'll have an easier time convincing them if you agree with their point of view every now and then. Show agreement by saying, *"I can see your point, and I agree that this is a cause for concern. However, I do believe..."* Validating their feelings tells them that how they feel matters to you, and that you are not merely trying to force your ideas upon them for your own benefit.

Finally, the most persuasive speakers always know when to step back. Trying to force anyone to agree with you immediately will do more harm than good. Take comfort in knowing that you have done your best, but at the end of the day, every audience member is a unique person with a mind of their own. They may be convinced – or they may not - but if you manage to pull off persuasion without being too forceful, most of your audience members should leave the room feeling agreeable with what you have just told them.

Using Body Language to Reinforce Your Points

Of all the public speaking techniques you have learned so far, your eye contact, tone of voice, and pauses during your speech are going to be the most helpful traits in this context. These skills, when performed correctly, will add more weight to your argument without you having to say the words out loud. Your body language is going to do much of the talking for you. The secret to successful persuasion is by focusing on *how or what you can do to be helpful to your audience.* That's what you need to aim for.

Most speakers, especially the new ones, tend to focus on how they can persuade their audience enough to get them to go along with their point of view. Instead, what they *really should* be focusing on is *how they can be helpful.* When you try to convince your audience from an angle that highlights the benefits of the solution that you are offering - addressing the needs of your listeners - it becomes much easier to get them to go along with your agenda.

People want to see what's in it for them, and when you can show them the ways they will benefit from your approach, they will be more than happy to hop over to your side without question. But do not forget you are not just trying to convince them with your words, you are trying to do it *with your body language*, too. Here's an interesting finding from a **University of British Columbia study (2013)** on the connection between eye contact and persuasion. The study found that in some situations, eye contact can produce significant help in situations where persuading another person is the goal. That said, keep in mind that in some circumstances, however, *too much* eye contact could cause your efforts to backfire. Instead of persuading your listener, you end up driving them away.

Eye contact has been mentioned several times already, and it makes another appearance here again because *it is so crucial* when you are communicating one-on-one or in a presentation to many people at one time. In short, effective personal communication cannot exist without the use of this essential process. You are going to have a hard time trying to persuade anybody if you can't even look them in the eye! Avoiding important eye contact may give them the impression that there is something fishy going on.

To be effectively persuasive, you are going to need to adjust the tone of your voice, too. When needed, you are going to have to change your vocal tone to effectively match the points and emphasis that you are trying to make. It's like tailoring the message to fit the audience you have in mind—except you are using your voice to do it. Your tone is going to depend on your context and the crowd that you are presenting to. If you are presenting to a group of colleagues at work, for example, then the tone you use should be professional and serious. Amongst general audience members, it can be jovial, upbeat, or a mixture of different emotions depending on the subject on which you are presenting. Avoid any language that sounds like it might carry an accusatory tone behind the message. Keep it neutral. Keep it professional. Most importantly, keep it to the point.

Another idea to keep at the forefront is that your audience may not always agree right away with what you are saying. Sometimes, they might not agree at all, and this might come up during the question and answer portion of your presentation. Your first instinct might be to get defensive, becoming immediately dismissive of their views, feeling the need to defend your views instead. That's not going to win you any points in the game of persuasion! You need to fight the natural tendency to jump to the defensive, taking a breath, using a pause, gathering your thoughts quickly before you respond. Remember to consider the tone of voice you are taking with your response. When you allow your audience to see that you are in control – even in situations sure to bring pressure to you – they will be impressed. This helps your listeners to warm up to your message even more (if they weren't already convinced before). Your tone takes precedence, in this case, as it can either win over your audience or cause an argumentative, heated debate; that is not how you want to end your presentation. Remember: eye contact, tone of voice, and pause. Use these together to create a winning, persuasive presentation.

The Importance of Knowing Your Audience

It will certainly help your persuasive efforts if you know and understand who you are talking to. Think of your presentation as if you are having a conversation with someone. The better you know the person, the more engaged, lively, and effective that conversational session is going to be. Knowing your audience works along the same principle lines. When you know who your audience is, it is easier to connect with them on an emotional level. This, in turn, makes it easier for you to persuade them because you have struck the right chord.

You *must* keep your audience in mind when preparing your presentation. If you do not understand your audience, how can they understand you? How will you convince to see why your presentation or speech can make a difference in their lives? Your goal is to show them that your solution is the answer that they have been searching for all along! Essentially, this is the goal of every successful communication: making yourself understood by others. You cannot expect listeners to understand you if you do not put them at the forefront of your mind as you prepare the content of your speech or presentation.

Think about the group of people you are speaking to. What kind of language would they respond to best? What types of words and vocabulary would they make the most connection with? What can you do to make your message resonate with them and make a lasting impression? Be sure only to use words that you are sure your audience is going to understand.

You wouldn't necessarily talk to your friends, family, co-workers, or acquaintances all in the same way. To be an effective and persuasive public speaker, you *must* be able to relate to the audience you are speaking to and make yourself more relatable to them, too. For example, you wouldn't use the same acronyms, slang or jargon on a particular group when you know they are not going to understand or can relate to it. But you might use it on *another group* that you must present to because *they can* relate and appreciate the use of these elements. The best public speakers out there never use the same material repeatedly, even if they are giving multiple presentations. The most effective public speakers tailor their messages to their targeted audience, becoming familiar with that audience before they give their presentation.

The best way to find out if your message was communicated effectively enough is to ask your audience directly during the Q&A segment. Feedback can go a long way in helping you determine places you need improvement. Was your message clear and easy to understand? If you have not convinced your audience, the Question/Answer segment provides you with the opportunity find out why - and the chance to try again. This feedback is going to be crucial towards your other presentations moving forward if you must give the same speech to another group of people.

Using Humor to Put Your Audience at Ease

Humor does not just help lighten the mood and make your presentation more interesting; it helps to put your audience at ease, settling them into a relaxed, comfortable state, opening them up to persuasion. An audience member who is stiff, on edge and tense has a hard time being convinced by what you are saying. Mentally, they have already put up an invisible barrier, making them less receptive to ideas.

Humor can be a great tool when used correctly. Of course, there could be risks involved with this approach, such as when inappropriate jokes or references are used. This is just one more reason that your speech should be tailored to the audience that you are going to address; knowing who your audience is critical to keeping your humor in line with their humor! If humor is risky, you might be wondering if it is a good idea to go ahead and use it in your presentations. The answer is yes—if you can, you should. Here's why the right kind of humor can be beneficial for your presentation:

- It relaxes both you and the audience. When the crowd is laughing along with you, it puts you at ease, alleviating some of the initial stress you might have felt at the start of the presentation.

- It makes you memorable. A public speaker who makes the audience laugh is one that is likely to be remembered instead of easily forgotten, as is the case with boring presenters.

- It bridges the gap between you and the audience. When you are laughing along with others, there is a sense of camaraderie that forms, and you feel almost as if you were friends. The ice is broken, and when everyone in the room is smiling, the atmosphere is visibly more relaxed.

- It captures your audiences' attention and keeps them interested. People are a lot more likely to listen closely to someone who is entertaining and funny.

- It makes you a much better speaker. Seeing your audience smile back at you will help you relax, allowing you to get comfortable enough to build a steady momentum when you are less worried.

- Public speaking can cause a great deal of anxiety for many speakers. But when you know that you have got what it takes to make your audience laugh, it can be a big help in easing some of that anxiety you feel. Hence, how do you use humor to your advantage and minimize the risks of it going south? You'll find these suggestions helpful:

- **Develop Your Own Anecdotes** - The best and most natural kind of humor stems from personal experiences. This kind of humor does not feel forced, which is good because then it does not seem like you are trying too hard. A possible low-risk option to play it safe would be to use a cartoon caption— if you can't think of any appropriate funny personal experiences to include.

- **Practice It on Others** - Before you present this delivery to a crowd, do a test run on a friend or family member, and observe their reaction. If they laugh the way you meant them to, then your audience is likely going to appreciate the joke, too.

- **Skip the Preview** - Humor should flow naturally as part of the conversation (or in this case, speech), so skip the preview and avoid the old, *"Here's a funny story" or "This is going to make you laugh."* Your audience can decide for themselves if your joke or story is funny enough. There's no need to announce that you are about to tell a funny joke or anecdote; it could backfire!

- **You Should Find It Funny** - Most importantly, you should find the joke or story funny, too. If you do not find it funny, it is likely your audience will not find it funny.

Chapter 9: You're Nearly There

A powerful speech comes down to the emotional value that it can offer the audience. It does not matter if your speech is 5-minutes, 20-minutes, or even an hour long. A 5-minute speech can be just as impactful as one that goes on for an hour if you know the essence of your message and deliver it effectively. When you find the essence, the crux, and the emotional value of your speech, that is when you can effectively gear your delivery and invoke an emotional response from your audience.

These are a few lessons that every public speaker should keep in mind to give powerful, emotional presentations every time:

- **Focus on the Problem Being Resolved -** This is a useful reminder when you are presenting on behalf of your company and trying to promote its products to your audience. A mistake made by a lot of speakers is to only focus on promotion, promotion, and promotion. While you may be doing what you are supposed to, this type of delivery puts audiences off. Focus instead on *showing them how to resolve the problems that they have*. Show them how the products are part of the puzzle, and how an effective solution you are offering can put those puzzle pieces together. Where possible, use personal examples of your own experience they can relate to.

- **Your First Words Must Count -** First words often provide the initial impact and impression you make when meeting someone new. As the old adage goes: "You do not get a second chance to make a good first impression." This applies to the first time you meet someone, and likewise applies to your upcoming speaking premier. Your opening matters because it sets the tone for the rest of your speech. How memorable you are on stage is dependent upon the those first, carefully chosen words you say. To leave your mark on the audience, be sure to give some thoughtful consideration to your opening: what would be the most compelling story with which to begin? What might provoke a strong emotional reaction in your listeners, causing them to sit up and pay attention from the start? Will you be a surprising speaker, or a predictable presenter? Will you be going the extra miles to find that unexpected opener?

- **Speaking to Your Crowd -** The essence of your speech is not to merely stand up there and reading all the lines you are supposed to. To deliver that emotional value, you need to speak to your crowd the way you would with your friends or family – people who you genuinely care about. You need to appear unpretentious to your listeners, considering them as an important audience to reach, not just sets of ears to which you are churning out facts. Facts may be helpful, but stories and emotions are the elements that will keep them actively engaged, making your speech memorable.

- **Let Your Passion Shine Through -** Passion is everything in an emotional delivery, and you must be genuine about it. When you love something and believe in it with all your heart, that is going to show, giving your speech the powerful, emotional delivery that no amount of pretense or rehearsals could ever give. Passionate speakers are obvious. When you authentically care, it is written all over your body language without you consciously remembering to watch that element of presentation. Passion must be the essence of your speech. Even the most mundane or dry topic can be utterly transformed if it is delivered by a passionate speaker.

- **Visualize Your Audience's Emotions** - To deliver a speech that really touches on your audiences' emotions, you need to *visualize the emotions you want them to feel.* What sort of emotions are you looking to invoke? What emotions do you want the essence of your speech to reflect? Once you have visualized the way you want your audience to feel, you can begin customizing your speech where each point that you make supports the emotions you are trying to invoke. Your audience may not be able to remember your exact speech word for word, but they will remember – for a long time – how your presentation made them *feel.* The best public speakers craft their presentations based on the emotions that they want their audience to feel at different segments of the speech.

- **Use "Grabbers"** - Want to make your audience feel at least one emotion or another throughout your speech? Use *grabbers* that pack an emotional punch right where they are going to feel it most. *Grabbers* are the few key phrases, statements, statistics, metaphors, or visuals that instantly "grab" the attention of your audience.

- **Make Your Content Emotional** - Don't focus on just delivering dry, mundane facts, and figures alone. You need to invoke the use of some thought-provoking, stirring sentiments in the phrases used throughout your speech. Emotions are going to be your most powerful weapon in any presentation. Yes, you need to deliver the facts, but instead of reading them to your audience, consider which phrases or key emotional words you can use to make the language more relatable to your crowd. If you want to make your audience feel something, you are going to have to use emotional words to back up your content.

- **Turning to Emotional Themes -** There are certain topics that have withstood the test of time and are still capable of invoking powerful emotional responses in your listener. Overcoming adversity, beating the odds, facing your fears, fighting for what's right, protecting the innocent, making a life-changing difference, heroic deeds; all are examples of emotional themes available for building your presentation. Look for ways you can naturally incorporate these themes into your speech.

- **Using an Emotional Tone -** You need to inject feeling and emotion into your voice and your tone, too, which is easy to do when you are passionate about your speech because it just comes naturally. It's easy to feel emotional when you are talking about a subject that you love. Your voice needs to reflect the emotional story that you are trying to tell. The right emotion and the right pauses during your speech can be powerful enough to bring tear to your audience's eyes. At the very least, look for stories that are appropriate to your subject and that will feelings deep within listeners.

- **Wrap It Up with A Punch -** Your conclusion needs to be just as powerful as your introduction was. Start with a bang and finish it with a bang. When you leave them with an emotional ending, your audience is going to say, *"Wow, that was incredible"* instead of thinking, *"I am SO glad that speech is finally over!"*

- More tips to keep your presentations as polished as possible include:

- **Don't Overdo the Words on Your Slide –** Many speeches include PowerPoint slides, giving your audience a point of reference. A common mistake made when using visual aids is making them too wordy. Your slides should only have the bare minimum text, choosing your words and visuals carefully. Are these the best possible representation of the essence of your speech? Condense and be concise. You do not need a lot of words on your slides – you just need *the right* words.

- **Act Natural Through Mistakes -** If you happen to make a mistake or two during your speech, act natural, keeping the smooth flow of your words; it's likely your audience will not notice! Mistakes are only obvious if *you make them obvious.* Don't be nervous, and do not let it little errors mess with your mind. Mistakes happen, that is okay. Just play it cool and keep moving forward. No one needs to know unless you want them to.

- **Cut It in Half -** Think about how much time you have been allocated to speak. Then, think about everything that you want to say and how much you think you can fit into the allocated time slot you have been given. Got it? Now, take all that content and reduce it by half. Do not be the type of speaker who tells their crowd they are running out of time, and even though there is a lot more they would like to say, they can't. Keeping your focus narrow and concisely delivering your message is key to a polished, professional speech. Your aim is to whittle your content in half so that you have time to spare, having a few other topics on hand to discuss - just in case. If you find that you have more time than you expected, consider bringing up the "back-up" topics. Keep in mind, though, that many audiences find themselves thrilled at the prospect of ending a little earlier than anticipated. Ending early is much better than having to announce that you have run out of time with plenty more to say! That scenario makes your presentation seem incomplete, and your audience may be unhappy without experiencing the closure they were expecting.

Bonus Tip: The Best Way to Begin Your Speech

Can't think of ideas on how to begin your speech? Try the following suggestions as an effective "hook" to reel in your audience. Start with:

- A question

- A statistic

- An emotionally shocking statement

- A quote

- A testimony

- A personal anecdote

- A story

- A visual

- Some natural humor

- Some sound effects

- A physical demonstration using an object

Putting It All Together

Everything that has been discussed so far *-the power of breath, pause, pace, eye contact, posture, gestures, tone, and pitch* - are elements, when combined, that will transform you into an outstanding public speaker. You will find yourself capable of persuasion, evoking emotion, as well as engaging and convincing your audience. This will happen even if you are nervous about it and even if you struggle with stage fright. It is inevitable that at some point during our lives, we will all be required to speak in public. It could be a presentation in college, at work, speaking in front of a crowd representing the company you work for, or even having to give a speech as an expert in your field. Public speaking skills are a necessity, and instead of expending energy trying to avoid it, why not channel that energy into brushing up on your skills instead?

It seems like there is so much to think about and remember, and that can feel a little overwhelming. But remember that you do not have to do everything all at once. It's okay to take it one step and a time and learn to master one skill before you move on to the next. Becoming a public speaker that is the envy of others is going to take time (and countless practice sessions), so do not be discouraged about having to go slow. It's better to go slow and do it right from the beginning than to try and do it all at once and stumble along the way.

Patience and hard work will go a long way. Oh yes, it is going to take *a lot of hard work.* Here's a recap of how to put it all together:

- **Start with the Eyes** - Eye contact is your best relationship-building tool up while on the stage. Use it to your advantage. Audiences respond to a speaker who is connecting with them through the eyes, and you present yourself as someone who is trustworthy and honest when you can sustain good eye contact throughout your presentation. Don't forget to move your gaze around the room in a steady, controlled manner so that you are not just focusing on one person alone. Your aim is to connect with as many people as possible. Eye contact should be anywhere from three to five seconds per person, or as long as it takes for you to finish one thought. If the thought is long, break it up by shifting your gaze to the next person. Avoid sustaining eye contact; this can make your listeners uncomfortable.

- **Hand Gestures Are Helpful** – (Not to mention effective.) Combine them with the rest of your body language and put it all together to emphasize your strongest points in the speech. Use your gestures for emphasis, but do not overdo to the point of distraction, making it difficult for your audience to focus. If you do not know what to do with your hands at times, the best rule of them is to steeple your fingers together until you arrive at your next point and your next set of gestures. Avoid putting anything in your pockets or holding on to any physical objects to minimize the risk of fiddling. If you do need to hold onto a pointer for your slides, do it so discreetly that your audience is barely aware of it. Never fiddle, this gives the impression of nervousness and impatience. Keep your palms open and facing the audience, so you present yourself as someone trustworthy with nothing to hide.

- **Perfect Posture -** Your posture represents confidence, so make tall, strong posture a part of your overall body language. Stand straight like you are trying to lengthen your spine as far as you can, and roll your shoulders back for the perfect, natural-looking confident posture. Avoid pacing on stage—this signals that you are nervous. Instead, aim for confident, well-timed strides at different intervals during your speech. If you must stand behind a podium or table, avoid leaning into these structures for support; doing so affects your ability to breathe deeply. If there is an option to avoid the podium, take it!

- **Emotional Facial Expressions -** Another body language element not to be overlooked is your facial expressions. Don't be afraid to use them to convey emotions, especially if you are trying to get your audience to feel just as emotional as you do. Keeping your expression strict and stony in a false attempt at professionalism will only backfire, making you seem aloof instead of relatable. If you are not conveying a range of emotions through your words and facial expression on stage, do not expect your audience to feel any kind of emotional connection to your speech either.

- **Remember to Vary Your Vocal Tone and Pace Yourself -** The *way you say it* matters just as much as what you say. You could be saying all the right things, but if your tone of voice falls flat and sounds uninspiring, it is not going to make much of a difference to your audience. Your tone is yet another tool that proves useful in striking an emotional response within your audience. If you want your audience to feel excited, your tone of voice should match the excitement *you feel*, the excitement *you want them to feel*. During the moments in your speech, which may be sad, let your tone of voice tell the story so that your audience feels just as emotional as you do. Simultaneously, your pace should be well-controlled throughout your entire presentation. Mono-speaking and monotone pace are not going to do you any favors in your quest to become a more effective public speaker. Speaking too fast puts you at risk of swallowing your words, and the last thing you want is to see your audience looking confused wondering what you just said! They will be too polite to interrupt, asking you to repeat or clarify the point.

- **Time Your Pauses -** Give your audience a chance to absorb your message fully with well-timed pauses throughout your presentation. Not only do you need to pace yourself, but you also need to know *when* you should stop speaking for several seconds. Public speaking is not a race, and if you have truly prepared and practiced, there is no reason to rush. You should prepare your presentation with ample time to deliver all that you need to - with time to spare. If you rush from one point to the next with no pause in between, it is going to be hard for your audience to keep up. Before they've even had time to digest the first bit of information you gave them, you are already rushing off to the next point. Pace yourself and pause, giving your audience the time necessary to process each point.

- **Key Takeaway Points**

- You must believe in yourself before others can believe in you as a speaker.

- Being a great speaker takes time and work, and it is going to take you several tries before you get it right.

- Never stop seeking feedback, even when you are great. There's always something that could use a little attention; there is always room for improvement.

- Appreciate all the constructive feedback you receive; the advice is meant to help you, not offend you!

- Build relationships with your audience before, during, and after your speech. Meet with them before your speech when possible. Communicate with your body language when you are on stage. Meet them after your presentation to seek feedback. The little things you do will go a long way towards making you a better speaker.

- Don't be afraid to show your audience your emotional side. They'll relate better to someone who's not afraid to make their passion than to a speaker who seems to be unapproachable.

- Make a genuine effort to connect with your audience. They'll respond well to sincerity.

- Making mistakes is not going to ruin your presentation completely. The way you handle yourself during and after those mistakes is the one that makes a difference.

- Forgive yourself if you make mistakes and take it as a lesson in stride. Even the best speakers out there have made some mistakes, so do not let it affect your confidence and weigh negatively on your mind.

- Stress-relieving exercises are going to make you a much better presenter if you use them beforehand. Less mental stress equals better on-stage performance.

- Always analyze your speech during your practice sessions and ask yourself how you can make it more engaging. Audience engagement is crucial to the success of your presentation. You can't call your speech a success if your audience is zoning out, barely remembering a word you have said.

- Listen to your audience and the concerns they raise during the Q&A portion of your presentation. Empathize with them and help them resolve the issues they face.

- Use humor in your speech to put your audience at ease. This opens them up to persuasion.

- Maintain the right body language all throughout your speech. Always stand straight and use diaphragmatic breathing.

- Avoid standing behind podiums or tables, as these create physical barriers between you and your audience.

- Share personal stories during your speech where possible—it is easier to invoke emotional responses from the audience when your stories come from the heart.

- Practice, practice, and then: practice some more - even when you think you have nailed it already. Repeat your performance in front of friend or family (or a mirror) until you know your content like the back of your hand, and until you have your pauses well-timed and your gestures on point.

Conclusion

Thank you for making it through to the end of this book! Let's hope it was informative and able to provide you with all the tools you need to achieve your goals—whatever they may be.

Hopefully, you feel better equipped to become the masterful public speaker you always hoped you could be. You *CAN* do this, even if you feel nervous and your heart is beating so fast like it might explode out of your chest! Public speaking is inevitable, so you might as well learn how to cope and equip yourself with the necessary skills you need to survive and thrive.

Public speaking is about more than just the words you say and the way that you are saying them. Giving a speech is an opportunity to build, foster, strengthen, and even explore new relationships that may lead to even greater opportunities. Public speaking only seems terrifying because we feel like we're going through it alone—but you are *not alone*. Your audience is there with you, and when you can connect with them, it creates a sense of belonging. Instead of thinking about it as having to present to a room full of strangers, talk to your audience as though you were talking to a friend.

The final rule to improving and mastering your public speaking abilities once and for all is to *let go of the past*. Think of this stage as your rebirth. You're about to become a whole new person, wiser, more emotionally intelligent, and someone who's going to eventually develop the confidence you need to stand in front of a crowd when you must. Let go of the past experiences you have had with public speaking, especially if they have been unpleasant. Like a snake, you are going to have to shed your old skin, leaving your past behind and embracing this new version of yourself. Leave your old worries at the door and move forward with everything you have learned today to become a better public speaker tomorrow.

If you found this book useful in your quest to become a better public speaker, a review on Amazon is always appreciated!

Part 2: Networking

Secrets to Highly Effective Small Talk, Persuasion, Conversation Starters, Emotional Intelligence, Body Language Habits, Influence, and Increasing Your Communication Skills with People

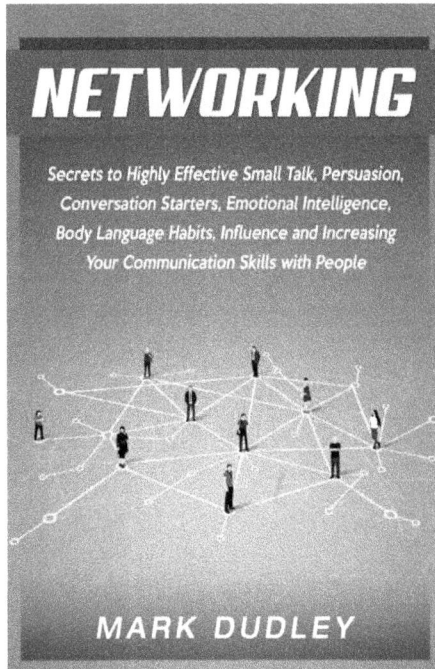

Introduction

As long as you are part of the working world—as a business owner, an entrepreneur, a tech analyst, a designer, a marketer, or even a physicist—you are bound to have done some form of networking, whether you realize it or not.

Business networking is a common and often must-do aspect of being an employee or business owner. You can't run away from it because as long as your job entails meeting people and forming connections, partnerships, and mutually beneficial relationships, you are part of the networking process.

But what is business networking anyway? In short, business networking involves establishing a mutually beneficial partnership with like-minded businesspeople, customers, clients, and suppliers.

For some people, business networking is second nature. They are effortless, confident, easy to talk to, can mingle with everyone and anyone, and can strike up a conversation on just about any topic.

But for some, it is a little hard, and this is absolutely normal. Not all of us are born with the gift of gab or even the gift of a social butterfly. You probably think you do not need to network, and you are right to a certain extent.

Some industries or employee levels do not require networking, or, rather, networking is not a priority. If you are in the tech development side where your job primarily involves machines and gadgets, you're probably better off spending more time on machines than on humans.

Or maybe if you are a designer whose focus is creating or bringing to life concepts and ideas given to you by your Creative Director or Team Lead (who would have done most of the talking with the client). It could also be your job is in the deepest remotes of the jungle and you need to collect species of plants and insects. You spend more time in a white lab coat than clicking a glass of martini at social events.

No doubt, some jobs and industries require fewer social interactions than others. But what happens when you need to speak to relevant parties for grant approval? Or maybe you need to mingle with the office crowd at your new job? What if you have been promoted and the new position requires you to ditch your lab coat and meet the board of directors to ensure your department or organization is well connected with philanthropists?

At some point, we need to create meaningful business connections to further our cause—whatever it may be, whether getting funds, getting a project approved, getting the right donors in, promoting your business, or even getting a raise.

This is when you start considering networking. In-person networking, even in the twenty-first century, remains among the best ways to ensure your career and business keep moving forward and you hit all your business goals.

People in any kind of industry and employment level are more likely to lend a helping hand or offer assistance if they know you personally. With a little preparation, you can definitely ace small talk and cement relationships with partners willing to be part of your cause.

You can attend various kinds of networking events and programs, depending on your goals in your career or business. While it may be difficult to start a conversation for someone who is introverted, various strategies and techniques can help you engage with the people you talk to and ensure the conversation is moving forward positively.

Why do you need to network, and what does networking involve?

Business networking enables you to leverage your personal and business connections to ensure your business continues to run and brings in growth and profits.

This concept is simple, but it involves relationship building, which takes time and is complex. It goes beyond just attending networking functions, shaking hands, drinking cocktails, and passing out business cards.

Take, for instance, two people attending an event, looking around sizing everyone up, and drawing an imaginary line to take over one half of the room. At the end of the event, they meet back and count the number of business cards each has collected.

Why collect business cards? What do they represent, and how are you planning to use them? Will these cards end up in a glass bowl or will you spam every one of those people with your company email newsletter?

A business card remains a business card unless you form a relationship. This is a strategy—a networking strategy turns a piece of card into an effective use of money, time, and energy.

The more you network, the more frustrations you may encounter simply because the progress is slow or there seem to be no fruits of their labor.

• Networking should be focused and strategic.

Not every person you meet can move you one step toward your goals, but the silver lining is everything *you* do can drive your business toward its goals. You can control who you meet and where you meet them and how deep you want to develop or leverage your relationships for business benefits.

• Networking requires you to be proactive.

The essence of networking is doing a specific activity each week geared toward business growth. You should be proactive in focusing on and planning your goals and be consistent in achieving these goals for each networking event.

You need to understand business networking to take up the challenge of looking for opportunities you may never have thought of (don't worry—we'll go through identifying this in other chapters). By understanding business networking, you can make invaluable investment decisions to ensure the steady growth of your business.

Are you ready for a Conversation?

Part of your journey toward business networking is creating your elevator pitch so you can describe succinctly and precisely what you do and who you are professionally.

You also need to do your homework before attending events to avoid wasting your time. Research the people attending your event to see the companies or groups in attendance. Check out their LinkedIn profiles if you can or even their company website. Take some notes so you know who they are, what their company does, or even the role they play in the company.

Other things you should and can do is check name tags during registration to see if you know the people there or the jobs they do. This will help you start conversations.

Business networking also entails deciding what to say and whether you have any interesting similarities.

How would you turn a quick introduction into an engaging and meaningful discussion? Once you do your homework, even if you are an introvert, business networking will become easier.

Are you ready to begin? Let's go!

Chapter 1—Understanding Business Networking and Its Benefits

Before we look into the where and how of business networking, it is important to know the benefits. Not only does it help you make the most of your time and effort, but it also helps remind you why you are doing this. Whenever you sign up for a networking event or join a mixer, remember the *why*.

The Professional Benefits

- **You get new contacts and referrals**

The most important benefit of networking is to meet potential clients, business prospects, donors, funders, suppliers, and investors. You also generate referrals with whom you can follow up and add to your client base. Networking enables you to identify plenty of opportunities for future joint ventures, partnerships, and possibilities to expand your business in different places.

- **Visibility**

One vital element for new businesses is to be seen and heard—people need to talk about them both online and offline. If you are a business owner, this is a crucial aspect of business success—to be in the minds of the right people. To ensure you are in the peripheries of your business relationships, you need to meet and communicate with your clients and prospects constantly. In other words, you need to maintain regular contact.

- **Staying Current**

Apart from visibility, you also need to stay current and be in the know for your industry. No matter what industry you are in, it is an ever-changing climate, and you need to stay updated with the market conditions, your target audience's needs, and the trends taking place. Staying abreast of your market ensures you develop successful marketing plans to address these changes, and networking is a great way to stay informed with your business associates and your peers.

- **Problem Solving**

Apart from increasing your business visibility to the right crowd, you would be surprised to know you can often find solutions to your business problems through networking. Say, for instance, your business needs a social media presence. You might find an ideal candidate or a reputable agency to handle this through your networking contacts. You can also find valuable investors and venture capitalists through your networking channels.

- **Knowledge & Experience Sharing**

Through your network, you can take advantage of your contacts' different viewpoints and past experiences. You can derive valuable info on good trade routes, import and export options in your industry, the best suppliers to work with, who to engage for web services and cybersecurity, and tips on expanding to international markets from someone in the same line of business as you. This saves you time and money, and it gives you an outlook on investing your time and money properly based on the feedback you receive from your network.

• Morale and confidence

Mentally, you need to surround yourself with optimistic, driven, and positive people, especially when you are running a business, establishing a start-up, or looking for a job. You want to associate yourself with people who can give you a morale boost when things are not looking so rosy, because the unprecedented usually happens in the world of business. You need to speak to people who have been through these phases and can advise you to plow through and what solutions you can implement. Regularly speaking to people can also boost your confidence, particularly if you are not naturally outgoing.

The Personal Benefits

• Friendship

Friendship plays an extremely important role in business networking. You might be thinking, "Nope, I'm here to create business connections, not make friends." But how many of you would be more available to help a friend compared to helping a business contact? If your answer is "friend," then you already know why forming friendships through business networking is important. You end up making friends with like-minded people through networking and realize both of you share common interests, passion, ideas, and business principles. Both of you might even come up with a brand-new idea for a business and venture out together. Who knows?

• Referral generation

An undeniable aspect of business networking is referral generation, which offers referrals pre-qualified for you. You can turn referrals into potential clients or reliable suppliers for your business. Business networking gives you the ability to reach out to quality leads with positive reviews from your networks.

- **Enhance your small talk skills**

We spoke about how business networking increases your confidence, and with more confidence, your ability to make small talk also increases, enabling you to connect with people you've never met before and form a conversation that could lead to more meaningful outcomes. Your business growth partially depends on creating connections and talking to people. If other business owners, clients, and suppliers find you easy to talk to and approachable, doing business with you is easier compared to a person who is hostile or hard to talk to.

Confidence in yourself also means you are confident in your business, and if you are confident in your business, this shows strength and reliability toward the people you connect with. They will be more likely to have you as a partner, client, or supplier because they feel your business is in good hands, you know what you are doing, and your business is profiting.

- **You get opportunities**

There is always an opportunity for growth at every networking event, depending on how you play your cards. Going in with a plan and an objective ensures you meet the right people and gain new opportunities. These opportunities can be anything from a new business idea, a new market segment, a new lead, a different angle for marketing, a potential client, or even a recruit. It could also be an opportunity to speak at a conference or be part of a round-table discussion. Whatever opportunities you follow must strengthen your business or personal goals; otherwise, you are just moving from one place to another with no real progress, whether personally or professionally.

In the world of business, it matters *who* you know and not *what* you know. Reliable connections are essential because they give you a wider pool to tap into.

- **Growing positively**

Networking also means creating a framework toward positive growth, professionally and personally. You need to learn from your mistakes and experiences. When you hit a stump or become frustrated with the direction of your business, your networks can pull you in and help you focus on the objective rather than dwell on your shortcomings. Positive connections you've built through networking can help you with this.

Bottom Line

With all the points mentioned in this chapter, you now have a firm understanding of how important it is to network, whether you like it or not. You ultimately want to increase your business revenue and become a better entrepreneur and businessperson, and networking with the right crowd will help you create these inroads in the world of business. So what are you waiting for? Let's start networking!

Chapter 2—Types of Networking Events to Attend

A big part of being skillful, confident, and networking with success is knowing what event you are attending, the kind of crowd, and what topic or the industry the networking event caters to.

Each networking event has its own objectives, and among these objectives is helping its attendees achieve their business goals. If an event does not have objectives and does not meet one or more of its target audience's goals, then the event is unsuccessful.

So why does this matter to you? Why is it important to know what you are signing up for when you register for a networking event?

First, it relates to time. Time is money, time is valuable, and you do not want to waste your time with an event that does not meet your networking goals and plan. Whether your plan is to excel in your career or expand your business connections, hitting the right event with the right participants is a valuable intangible asset to the foundations of your goals.

What Are Networking Events?

Almost every event is an opportunity to network if you play your cards right, but networking events are specifically geared toward enabling attendees to engage and connect with like-minded individuals. These aren't just confined to types of gathering but any setting that enables people to find valuable connections.

Types of Networking Events

Industry and Career Fairs

Fairs are an excellent place to see and get to know the players in your industry and the big names recruiting. Both career and industry fairs give attendees the opportunity to seek better connections or job offers. For career fairs, employers may be on the lookout to recruit for specific job opportunities or even connect with attendees to both provide and gain information. Career and industry fairs are usually busy, with carefully laid out halls, and things move fast. If you are on the lookout for a job or even a business opportunity, be sure to practice your elevator pitch before you go so you know what to say to future employers and business partners.

Chamber of Commerce Events

The Chamber of Commerce usually organizes regional events, from workshops to mixers and fundraisers for networking purposes and for local charities. These functions and events give you an excellent opportunity to meet both local employers and industry players, potential clients, and suppliers. When you attend these events, perfect your elevator pitch and have enough business cards to hand out. In the twenty-first century, most business cards come with QR codes so your potential client or partner can immediately scan them and get a direct link to your website or even LinkedIn page.

Church Groups

Church groups may be the last place you would think of networking for both career and business prospects. Church groups offer an environment where you can casually network with people who hold a common spiritual belief. You know them in a different light because you have probably worked with them on church activities such as a church bake sale, coffee after services, or even church charities.

College Alumni Programs

Colleges often sponsor non-career related events, which gives alumni, employers, and business owners a chance to meet and network over a common interest. Non-career events include museum tours, gallery visits, exhibitions, exhibitions related to industries, and sporting events. Alumni can connect informally, taking off some pressure to impress. However, you must still be professional and exhibit good conduct. These mixers and events usually lead to informal business meetings and interviews, so be ready to share your business goals and career status when the conversation fits.

College Career Networking Events

College networking events offer the opportunity to meet other industry players and potential employees from a large group of graduates and alumni. Events like this take place on campus grounds or even in cities with a significant alumni population. The common denominator in these events is the opportunity to introduce yourself as a prospective employee or even a prospective business associate.

Speed networking is usually a popular structure at these types of events since hundreds of alumni and students and business partners are present and you can work the rounds.

Community Service Groups

Another popular choice for networking is through community service groups such as the Leo Club or the Rotary club. This gives you an outlet to meet volunteers and staff fundraisers and attend other events where you can also interact with donors. Your common shared interest in charitable tendencies can connect your interests and put you in a favorable position among potential partners and employers.

Another way is to join a service group and build your network among other community members. While expanding your network is your agenda, it is equally important to be part of community projects you are passionate about because your passion will show. Lack thereof shows insincerity.

Diversity Groups

You can also join groups based on gender, ethnicity, or race, such as the Young Men's Christian Association or even the Society of Black Engineers. These groups recognize the value of networking, and they usually integrate this aspect into their events, activities, and lectures.

Job Club Meetings

You can join geologist clubs or artist clubs; you get to meet other club members who can provide connections to suppliers, donors, investors, and even give you job referrals and leads. Joining job clubs is an extremely effective way to network because you get direct connections to industry connections.

Professional Conferences

Finally, we'll discuss networking in professional conferences. These events are usually organized by trade associations and include both formal and informal networking components. You get to be part of meetings, roundtable discussions, workshops, and mixers. You can volunteer to organize these conferences apart from just being an attendee because then you can evaluate the other attendees and their work style and can build your own skill set.

Chapter 3—Creating a Networking Plan

Networking, as we all know now, is not only confined to business meetings, corporate parties, and conferences. As long as you put yourself out there where other people are, you are already kick-starting a networking process. You'd be surprised how some of the most ordinary places can become a place to exchange business information, like the gym or even a dog park.

The people you meet at the coffee shop, at the Pilates class, the grocery store you always frequent, or at town hall meetings are all suitable networking opportunities. The best part is you already have a common shared interest.

The essentials of successful networking begin with good foundations. As long as you know exactly what you want to gain, where to look for the people you want to network with, and where to display yourself, you will achieve success and make full use of your time and energy.

So how do you network successfully? The first thing to do is create a network plan—a simple framework to identify what to do, where to do it, and how to do it. If you do not have the gift of gab, have problems connecting with people, or just have trouble talking with ease, a networking plan is essential. However, having a networking plan is always a good idea even if you have no problem communicating or you are a pro at it. It prepares you for the situation you are getting into.

What Are the Effective Networking Strategy Plans?

Networking sounds easy, doesn't it? You just show up at events and talk to strangers? Saying it is one thing but attempting it is another story altogether. When networking is done poorly, you not only waste time but also energy and even resources. Networking is a lot trickier than you think, and without proper planning, you end up representing your company and image in a bad light.

In the world of networking, the sharpest sword is word of mouth—it can be used for you and against you. Even when you have a solid business plan for the next five years of growth, it will not be sufficient to acquire strong foundations for success. Your plan must include networking with the right people at the right events. It is not only about making new connections but deepening the ones you already have.

In this chapter, we will help you create a networking plan so you know what to target, who to target, when to network, and what to say.

- Determine your networking goal

No plan can be successfully carried out without a clear indication of a goal. Goals help us focus on our vision, objectives, and purpose. You need a networking goal if you want to have a successful outcome, so before you register for the next business mixer, ask yourself why you need to do this. If you do not figure out what you want to achieve, you will never create the right strategies to help you achieve these targets.

So what are your goals? Here are a few questions to ask yourself when you see a prospective networking opportunity:

- Am I networking to get new businesses and contacts?
- Do I want to build new relationships?
- Will I be meeting my current contacts at this event?
- Can I get a reliable mentor or sponsor at this location?
- How can this event broaden my career prospects?
- Is this the right event to create a positive image for myself and my brand?
- Is this event the right place to gain a team of experts?
- Can I increase my knowledge through this event?
- Can I gain new ideas by attending this workshop?
- How can I better my performance through this event?

When you know what you want to gain, you can proceed with a plan.

- Determining the number of people you will network with

Meaningful networking takes time. Once you strike a conversation with someone, it will take a while to pry yourself away and move on to the next person—less time if the conversation is stale. Networking does not mean you can approach someone and rattle off every detail about yourself or your business. You need to establish rapport first and start with a small talk, which can be time consuming.

When you sign up for a networking event or soiree, create a limit for yourself. Decide how many people you can speak to during the event. Having a target number of people to speak to enables you to ensure every connection you make is meaningful and memorable. You may have a few reasons for networking at a specific event, and you can create a different number for each reason. Prioritizing makes it easier to work the room.

Sometimes your main priority could be to reach out to new contacts, but then you find yourself at an event with few prospects and find you have a better chance of networking with investors for your upcoming project. You should be smart with your timing when networking to cover enough ground to hit some of your goals.

- Finding out who the attendees are and who to network with

Finding out who the attendees are saves you so much time! One way to find out who will be in attendance is by checking social media to see if anyone you know will be there. List all the people who will be helpful in pursuing your goals. You can work your way around the room by meeting the people you intend to connect with first.

If the person you want to network with is someone new, you might need to find a common bridge to talk about. Therefore, finding out the attendees ahead of time is a great idea. Also, identify the target companies and organizations that will attend so you have a substantial pool to work with.

- Review and act upon it

None of the above steps in your networking plan will come to fruition if you do not review your performance and act upon it. You need to turn your networking plan into an action plan. Once you have all the details you need, review them after each networking session. Edit your plan so you can work out any kinks for future networking opportunities.

Identify whether you have achieved your purpose or goals and your next action plan. Are you calling your contacts? Sending them an email? How are you establishing your next move? Did they invite you for a lunch meeting to talk things over? Did one of your contacts ask you to email them your proposal? Did they recommend you check out a website?

Next, for each person you spoke to, identify what the outcome was and your next step. Do not put it off for too long. You want to act upon your action steps as soon as possible.

Since you have identified your networking plan, it's time to look into the mirror and see yourself—who you are, what your strengths are, and what can you do to increase your confidence and gain better communication skills.

Chapter 4—Identifying Your Personality

Have you done any personality quizzes lately to identify who you are as a person? It is fun to see what our hidden personality traits are and what are our likes and dislikes are. Some online quizzes are fun, but some of them usually reveal aspects of our behavior, which we never thought even had a name.

These personality tests help shed some truth and wisdom on our preferences, behavior, and personality and give meaning to the way we do things, the way our brain works and how we relate to the things happening around us.

Doing a personality quiz can be an extremely useful exercise to get to know yourself a little better, whether it is about finding out which pasta fits your personality type or a serious psychological inventory. Plenty of personality quizzes exist, but if you truly want to find out your personality type and the strengths and weaknesses related to that type, take a legitimate psychological assessment based on science.

Among the most popular is the Myers-Briggs Type Indicator (MBTI). People who have taken this test say it has helped them gain a better understanding of themselves.

The MBTI was created to assess the psychological inclination of how a person views the world, how they interact in it, and what influences them to make decisions in their lives. The MBTI method was developed by the mother-daughter team of Isabel Briggs Myers and her mother, Katharine Briggs, based on the research and personality theories created by psychoanalyst Carl Jung. This assessment has been used frequently by career counselors, psychologists, in team-building seminars, and employers. It provides a quick way to figure out more about a person and how they fit in certain roles.

Would personality assessments help in becoming a better communicator?

The short answer is yes and no. Knowing your personality offers plenty of benefits but doesn't necessarily make you a better communicator. Knowing your strengths and weaknesses enables you to understand what you are good at and what you are not and make sense of why you are who you are. But to become a better communicator, you need to also work on your communication skills and social ethics by reading and being up to date with what's happening around you.

Finding out various aspects of your personality is just one step toward becoming a better communicator.

Benefits of Personality Tests

- Knowing Your Personality Type Can Help You Understand People Better

After seeing your results from an MBTI test, you will have a better understanding of the different perceptions and reactions of the people around you toward the same situations. You will have a better idea of why someone gets stressed out easily and why someone else is cool and calm—we all have a different view of interacting with the elements around us.

You will also see plenty of different personality types and one is not better than the other. We are all just different, and each person with a different personality brings something interesting and new to the team or conversation.

People mistakenly think everyone is the same and we all share the same views, attitudes, opinions, and traits. When we take a personality test, we often see our own personal preferences highlighted, and we get a glimpse of other people's traits as well. Understanding our core personality traits and those close to us helps us create meaningful relationships.

For example, if you are an extrovert and your colleague is an introvert, you will spot the signs of exhaustion or the need to take a break from socializing. You will also understand why they are quieter than you are.

- It Can Help You Identify Your Likes and Dislikes

You may hate talking in front of a huge audience but can hold your ground in a small table talk discussion, but you never understood why. By doing a personality test, you learn your extroversion or introversion range, and you will also understand why you like some things and why you do not like certain things. This is crucial to understand because it helps you make important decisions in your life, such as which job to take, which business opportunity works for your current industry, or even which college major to focus on.

Selecting an opportunity, profession, or major aligned well with your personal preferences will make you happier, passionate, and more satisfied with your job, your career progression, your business growth, and overall life.

- You Can Understand Which Situations Allow You to Perform Your Best

When you learn more about your personality type, you can also discover new approaches to the problems you have been experiencing. For example, if you find out you have a higher introversion range, work on putting more time into situations new to you. When you join networking events, prepare yourself even more to find out what the event is about, who's coming, and what to say so you do not get tongue-tied. Understanding what works best for your type will open you up to new ideas on solving problems, coping with conflict, dealing with stress, and managing several projects.

- You Can Better Understand Your Strengths and Weaknesses

This is the most important aspect of a personality test—figuring out your strengths and weaknesses, and this is ideal for a variety of situations in life. Knowing what you are good at and what you are not good at can also help you decide what kind of networking events you thrive in.

Maybe you're better suited to networking scenarios in a church group, for example. Or maybe you thrive in a corporate networking event that involves rapid-fire presentations. Maybe you are at your best at musical events, such as an opera or musical. You may have strong organizational skills and be a detailed-oriented person, which makes it easy for you to be part of programs like fundraisers.

- Remember Personality Tests Have Limitations

Knowing your type does not necessarily mean this is the be all and end all of who you are. Don't let this test define you as a person. Personality tests help you understand who you are, but they do not tell you what you can accomplish or how you perform in certain situations or even who you can be in the future. You may be an introvert now but with training and exposing yourself to various social situations, you can break out of your shell. You will find you can, in fact, talk easily with people—all you needed was a little practice.

You should not let yourself be defined by the elements in this test. You should not skip presenting a project because your test says you are an introvert. Don't give yourself the excuse of "I am an introvert; I do not do well in presentations."

Some reasons you might not want to take the results of all these personality quizzes too seriously:

- Your personality type does not tell you if you will love a specific career or succeed in a job.

The test just gives you an idea of the areas that appeal to you and the industries you may thrive in, but there is a huge difference between being interested in a certain field and enjoying the actual job. For example, your test may say you are great with numbers, so a job as an accountant would be great, but you might find this job is not as fulfilling as you thought.

- It may keep you from trying new things.

If your test says you are an extrovert, the common perception is you would reject quiet or solitary activities. When this happens, you end up missing out on experiences you can learn from or discovering such a working environment could be more conducive for you to come up with new ideas.

You could also end up missing out on meeting the right people when it involves quieter networking events, such as a gallery visit or a silent auction, just because they do not share the same traits as you.

Do not be too hung up on labels—whether it is the personality test or something else altogether. Do not limit yourself to your type. Explore as much as you can and try different things, even if it against your type.

- The test may prevent you from forming authentic relationships with people who do not share the same traits as you.

If you stick hard and fast to the ideas set in your personality type, you will reject those who do not fit your type. The beauty of people lies in their diversity, and people different from you can offer you a significant lesson. Excluding people just because they are different from you will make your view restricted, which is not a situation you want if expanding your business or advancing your career are your goals. Not only that, it restricts your social circle.

Bottom Line

Personality tests, whether real psychological assessments or fun quizzes taken online, can open a window into your personality and give you insightful views of what you like, do not like, the experiences you thrive in, and the kind of person you are.

But never let them define you and cause you to restrict yourself from exploring new things, new ideas, new situations, and things outside your comfort zone. Our personalities are stable overall, but this does not mean our lives are static. We grow and change over time, and the things we learn and experiences we go through makes us better people overall.

Chapter 5—Building a Better Persona

What happens when a conversation doesn't pique your interest? As polite as you may try to be, eventually you'll just drift off and lose interest, forgetting what you were talking about as soon as the conversation is over.

Understandably, making conversation can be difficult, especially if you're not a naturally social person by nature. You're worried you may have nothing to say, or you may have nothing in common with the person you're speaking too. Maybe you're even worried the conversation could bore the other person.

Here's a little secret to start you off – want to know what it takes to make a conversation great? *Timing.*

Your timing is everything, even when it is just small talk. Never barge into the middle of a conversation when the person you want to approach is already in discussion with someone else or is busy. They're distracted, most likely annoyed at being interrupted, and they won't give you their full attention. Forget any hopes of being interesting; you won't even hold a proper conversation.

Five Effective Techniques Will Make You More Interesting During a Conversation

#Technique 1: Remember Their Names – When the other person introduces themselves to you, make a habit of repeating their names to increase your chances of remembering who they are. For example, if the person says, *Hello, I'm John*, you should respond, *It's nice to meet you, John; I'm Jane.*

The immediate act of repeating someone's name will help the memory stick with you. When you can recall their names, they'll automatically warm up to you and be more inclined to hold a conversation. Nothing is less appealing than having someone say, *I'm sorry, what was your name again?* Especially after they've already introduced themselves.

#Technique 2: Ask Open-Ended Questions – Small talk should be a two-way street, and if you keep your questions open-ended, you're on the right track to doing just that. Ask questions that encourage the other person to open up and share more information about themselves. Steer away from questions that tend to put the conversation at a dead-end, because you will only be left with an awkward silence, wracking your brain for what to talk about next.

Asking questions that encourage the conversation to flow and develop naturally is the best practice.

#Technique 3: Offer a Compliment But Be Genuine – Never underestimate a person's ability to spot a fake person a mile away. While offering a compliment is a great way to break the ice and start small talk with a stranger, don't do it unless it's genuine. Being fake will only make you appear dishonest, insincere, and like you are trying too hard to curry favor.

Remember the old saying *If you can't say something nice, don't say anything at all?* Make it your mantra when attempting to make small talk. If you offer a compliment you don't mean, your words may say one thing, but your body language will convey a whole different story. If you want people to view you as someone who is interesting enough to strike a conversation with, be sincere right from the beginning.

#Technique 4: Actively Participate – Small talk, like any other conversation, takes two to tango. Don't start a conversation but eventually decrease your participation and let the other person do all the talking. They will get tired of you quickly and move onto a person they can have a better conversation with. If you want to be interesting throughout the entire process, you must be an active participant.

Be an active participant by listening and paying attention when the other person is speaking so you can follow up appropriately. This helps stimulate a healthy conversational flow, and you will win points with the other person because they will be eager to talk to you when they feel they are being listened to and heard.

#Technique 5: Know What's Going On – The more you know about what is going on in the world around you, the better conversationalist you will be. You should be prepared for small talk to revolve around discussions about the current events in the world, and not just confined to business talk or idle chit-chat about random things. The more prepared you are, the more knowledgeable you will appear to be, and the more interesting you will become to the people with whom you're speaking.

Make it a habit daily to check the news headlines each morning, read many books on a diverse range of subjects, and scan the internet for the latest topics and trends. This information will allow you to become a much better participant whenever you're having small talk with just about anyone because there's always something you can connect to.

Key Takeaway Points:

- Timing is crucial to start a conversation on the right foot.

- Remember their names.

- Keep your questions open-ended to encourage conversation flow.

- Be genuine with your compliments (never fake it).

- Be an active participant (listen and respond).

- Increase your general knowledge.

Chapter 6—Building Confidence

Confidence will help you handle small talk a lot easier if you have it. When you're confident, you feel like you have the power and ability to do anything in the world. Nothing seems impossible when you view it with a confident and positive mind. Have you ever had that feeling?

It happens with small talk too. Those who can handle small talk like they've been doing it their whole lives seem to ooze confidence and charm. Talking to a perfect stranger doesn't make their palms sweat, and during a conversation, they never seem nervous, jittery, or anxious.

Self-confidence isn't innate for many people. Some people are born with it; some people have to work for it. But that's the good news though; you *can* work on it and it can be developed, just like small talk.

If you've ever thought to yourself, *I wish I had that kind of confidence,* well, good news! You're about to learn the secrets and become one of those smooth-talking operators you so admire.

Five Effective Techniques to Help You Build the Confidence You Need

#Technique 1: Change Your Mind – Change your mind and you will change your life. It's true. Understandably, being negative seems to come a lot easier, but if you want to start building a confident personality for yourself instead of just admiring it in others, you must change your mind. This means slowly getting rid of negativity.

Start by taking it one day at a time. When you wake up every morning, commit to saying you will make it through the entire day without being negative and see how well you do. In the beginning, you're bound to slip up occasionally, and that's okay because, eventually, it gets easier and easier each day until you finally reach a day when you've made it without being negative even once.

Successful people always preach about one core concept, which is to cultivate a positive mind. See the silver lining in the situations you go through. Evaluate those closest to you—are they a positive influence or are they negative influence? Keeping a close circle of positive people is essential to making this technique effective. Be positive, even if you don't feel like doing it, do it. Do it until it becomes second nature to you.

#Technique 2: Visualize – Napoleon Hill once said, *If you can see it in your mind and believe in it, then you can achieve it.* Never has a truer word (or sentence, in this case) been spoken. Visualization is such a powerful tool, which, unfortunately, often gets underestimated. But think about this—if you can visualize all the bad scenarios and believe in them so much they are strong enough to stop you from doing something, why can't it work the other way around?

If you can visualize the negative, then you can visualize the positive. If you want to build up the confidence to make small talk with any stranger, you must start focusing more on the positive visualization aspect. Visualize yourself as a confident person, a person who is interesting and a person people want to talk to, whenever you're in a room or a gathering. Visualize yourself thriving in every conversation and cement the image strongly in your mind until it starts to manifest itself.

#Technique 3: Preparation – Confident people are that way because they're prepared. Remember that you can work on and gradually build up confidence? Well, one of those "works" involves being prepared. Before you can master the art of small talking at the spur of the moment, you will need some practice to work up to it.

You get practice by preparing yourself before you have to meet people. Before a potential business or client meeting, a gathering, or an event where you would mingle with a group of strangers, chances are you'll have some advance notice *before* you attend the event, right? Mentally prepare yourself. Technique 1 and 2 come in handy because you need to view meeting people as a positive thing instead of dreading it like you normally would. Then visualize yourself confidently and expertly handling each conversation with any person you're likely to meet.

#Technique 4: Adopting the Equality Mentality State of Mind – Nothing is a bigger confidence killer than thinking someone is better than you are and wishing you were more like them. This common pattern can be seen in those who suffer from low self-esteem, which is why they tend to shy away from others and beat themselves up all the time by constantly thinking they're never good enough or never will be as good as someone else.

Why compare yourself when no two people are similar? You have your own strengths, and they have theirs. It doesn't mean one person is better than the next; it simply means we have all gone through different experiences and learning scenarios, which have shaped us to be the person we are today. If you want to build your confidence, you need to get rid of this perception you're not as good as other people.

Instead, remind yourself everyone is equal. Everyone has something to offer, including you. Shift your perception and start believing everyone is equal.

#Technique 5: Stop Beating Yourself Up – Last but not least, you need to learn to tune out and eventually eliminate the inner critic within you if you want to build your confidence. Everyone's got an inner critic, which can be your own worst enemy. The difference between confident people and those who struggle with confidence is the confident ones have learned to get rid of their inner critic because they know it is self-destructive.

It is impossible to love yourself or even feel remotely confident when your inner voice keeps harping on the negative. If the negative things about yourself are the only thing you can focus on, you have little hope of ever building up any kind of self-confidence.

Whenever you feel yourself heading in that direction, learn to immediately put a stop to it and just say no—you will not give in to your inner critic today. It helps if you can focus on other things and distract yourself whenever the inner critic rears its ugly head. To truly become the confident person you want to be, you need to stomp your inner critic out of existence so it can no longer threaten to bring down your self-esteem.

Key Takeaway Points:

Before you can begin charming anyone like a million bucks, you first need to charm the most important person of all – yourself. When you're confident, no challenge you face will ever bring you down, including the challenge of making small talk with perfect strangers.

- Visualize yourself as a confident person.

- Get rid of negative thoughts and people if needed.

- Get rid of the inner critic within that threatens to disrupt your self-esteem.

- Nobody is superior to you; everyone is equal.

- Mentally prepare yourself before any situation to make small talk with people easier to handle.

- Change your mind and you will change your life.

- Write down things you like about yourself to help you focus on the positive.

- Love yourself.

Chapter 7—Building Charisma

What's another thing you notice about people who can make small talk like this is what they were born to do their entire lives? Confidence is part of it, and they seem to have something else that also begins with a C–Charisma.

Hang on, isn't charisma something some people are born with, which is why they are more likable than others? Yes and no. Yes, some people are naturally charismatic individuals, but if you're not, there's no reason you can't become one of them.

What can you say about charismatic people? They're likable, but you can't quite explain precisely *why* they are so likable. They have a certain *je ne sais quoi* you just can't quite put your finger on. They seem to have an aura that flows out of them, which people become drawn to. That's the magic of charisma.

Many people mistakenly think charisma is part of your nature and who you are as a person, not realizing it is actually more about the way you carry yourself and the things you say and do. You can create charisma for yourself. One of the many secrets and techniques of successful people is that, just like everything else they have, they put in the work. They built up their charisma if they weren't naturally born with it. Why? Because they knew it could be done.

Five Effective Techniques to Build Charisma

Just like confidence, building charisma will take some work, but adopting these five techniques will give you a good head start:

#Technique 1: Being Present – Tying in closely with confidence is mastering the art of being present, which is an important part of becoming a more charismatic version of yourself. When you're making small talk with another person, attempt to be present, be there wholeheartedly, and truly engage with the person. Being present instantly makes you more likable in the other person's eyes because you're showing them they are important enough to have your complete and undivided attention.

Giving your full attention to a person is important because you may think you've done a good job of hiding your inattention, but the truth is you haven't. Body language is more powerful than you give it credit for, and when someone isn't fully paying attention to you, it shows. Charisma is about being likable, and by being present, you make the other person feel good about themselves because nobody likes feeling ignored or not important enough for you to hold a conversation with. Don't engage in small talk if your mind is on something else and you're distracted. Be there, be present, and be engaged.

#Technique 2: Mastering the Basics of Conversation – Charismatic people are so likable because they know how to talk to people in just the right way. They know how to make others feel comfortable during a conversation, they know how to start and carry a conversation, and they are in control and able to steer the conversation in a positive direction so everyone feels good at the end.

This means you must learn to master the basics of conversation, which means you *must* talk to people at the most basic level;

otherwise, you're doomed to fail right from the start. A good way to learn how to connect with people on a basic level? Be nice.

Don't try to show-off during a conversation; don't be boastful. Don't start with jokes, especially if you're meeting someone new because you could risk appearing inappropriate. Keep it simple; be nice. Be sincere and show a genuine interest in the person. Attempt to connect on their level, share experiences and encourage them by asking open-ended questions.

This will take practice, so don't worry and don't stress if you don't get it right away. It will feel awkward and difficult in the beginning, but, eventually, you'll get the hang of it.

#Technique 3: Just the Right Amount of Eye Contact – Charismatic people have the confidence to make eye contact with the people they're speaking to. And you know they are confident because when they talk, their eyes are never downcast or shifting elsewhere like they are looking for an escape. They're confident, they're in control, and they connect with you by looking you in the eyes when engaging in conversation.

Eye contact is an important conversational tool because they can communicate more effectively than words do. When you're angry with someone, you communicate by giving them an icy glare, and there's nothing friendly about your eye communication at that moment. When you're in love, you look into your partner's eyes with love and tenderness. When you have something to hide, or you're uncomfortable, you avoid making direct eye contact with anyone.

Eye contact reflects sincerity, and it sends the message to the person you're talking to you're interested in them and what they have to say. When you make them feel important and interesting, they automatically like you more because everyone likes to be heard. Starting to realize the secret of charisma yet? You become more likable by making *other* people feel good.

#Technique 4: Think Before You Speak – Charismatic people understand it is important to think before you speak to avoid putting their foot in their mouth. One wrong word or sentence is all it takes to instantly put people off. Once that happens, it is often an uphill battle to regain favor in their eyes. Charismatic people know this, which is why if you want to become a more charismatic person, you must emulate what they do and think about everything you're about to say before it leaves your mouth.

Yes, even during small talk. These conversations will leave a lasting impression about you, about the way you've carried yourself, and the things you said. Your mind should be working twice as fast to process the information you're receiving from the other person. Before you speak, quickly analyze what you plan to say to make sure it's appropriate. Once spoken, words can never be taken back, which is why it is so vital for anyone who wants to win at small talk to understand this crucial point.

#Technique 5: Smile – One of the most important qualities charismatic people have is a warm, friendly, and approachable nature. They demonstrate this by doing one simple thing—smiling. A smile can magically transform people and situations in ways we cannot even imagine, and it makes a world of difference. When you smile, it instantly lights up your face; people immediately feel more comfortable and at ease around you, and they end up smiling in return.

A sincere smile is the most effective way to convey warmth and is perceived as one of a person's most positive attributes. So when starting small talk, begin on the right note with a warm and sincere smile, and you will be amazed at how people respond.

<u>**Key Takeaway Points:**</u>

Being charismatic is about becoming a more likable person who oozes a positive aura, which makes people gravitate toward you. You do this as follows:

- Be present in the situation (don't let your mind wander elsewhere)

- Give your full attention to the person you're talking to.

- Learn to connect with people on a basic level.

- Be nice and be sincere in attempting to connect with others.

- Maintain good eye contact.

- Charisma is not about you; it's about making other people feel good .

- Think before you speak.

- The things you say will leave a lasting impression of you.

- A sincere smile can do wonders for your personality.

Chapter 8—Building a Positive Mindset

Have you ever found yourself in this kind of scenario?

You have your networking goals, or, at the least, you have a goal in mind when you attend an event or workshop. You craft a well-thought-out networking plan, you write what you want to say, and you identify the people you want to talk to at this event. You are dressed for the event, your hair is brushed and teeth clean, and you feel like you're reading to take on the world…

Suddenly, you get anxious and overwhelmed, feeling you haven't prepared, and start thinking of everything that could go wrong. You start perspiring, your palms get sweaty, and you are worried. Then you find yourself unable to walk out the door to go to the event.

Have you been through this before?

Chances are you have. Our thoughts get the better of us, and we question our abilities and our strengths even though we've trained so hard for this moment.

It's ok to suddenly feel anxious or worried—we are humans, after all, with a wide emotional range. Now if your willpower is strong, you will mentally give yourself a pep talk and tell yourself to calm down, take a few deep breaths, and start thinking more positive things like all the things that will go right.

But what happens when our willpower isn't so strong and we cave in to all the negative talk in our heads? This is where the power of a positive mindset comes into action. Our mind is the only thing stopping us from doing great things, and this is within our control to nurture.

We can work on our confidence, our persona, and our charisma, but all these elements are futile without the right mindset.

Mind over Matter

Your mindset will determine how you behave and how successful your encounter will be. When we meet new people, it is common to be a little self-conscious and have a heightened self-awareness of what is going on with ourselves, what is happening around us, and whether we are being assessed by others.

This is, however, not the most effective way to socialize or create successful communication and networking. Excessive self-consciousness makes us more anxious and less confident, and sometimes when we are at the center of interaction, we end up being unable to be empathetic to what the other person feels. You might feel invigorated by your conversation, but the other person may have felt dull and bored.

When this disconnect occurs between how you feel and how the other person feels, it will reduce your chances of establishing a positive influence and improving your social skills. What's worse is if you feel unsure of yourself and question your abilities, the other person will 'feel' this energy coming from you.

So what do you do?

Part of networking or negotiating successfully and having good communication skills is having a positive mindset. You may have the right plan, the right words, and the right attitude, but you also need a strong sense of positivity to help you pull through if the conversation doesn't go your way or you're asked a question you cannot answer. How do you maneuver from a situation like this? Let's look at some ways we can exercise our mind to be more positive so we can prevent situations where we feel dumbfounded or insecure or even say the wrong things when we are flustered.

1. First steps to a mentality change

To positively influence a person or a group of people, you need to change your mentality toward becoming positive too. Changing our mindset to be positive requires manifesting it in our minds. With positive emotions, you will see more possibilities in life. They broaden our possibilities and thinking, thus opening up more options for us in facing issues, crises, problems, and solutions. In the next few chapters, we will discuss how we can look at things in a more positive perspective to enhance and give more value to our life, relationships, and goals. It is not as hard as it seems because all it takes is a little practice.

Positive thinking is applied in many fields, from business to sales, marketing to advertising, health, sports, education, motivation, inspiration, psychology, and self-image. Many twenty-first-century authors apply positive thinking in various areas. Some of them include:

- Anthony Robbins' seminar and speeches using the knowledge of psychology and positive thinking. Robbins' is a motivational speaker and advisor to many world leaders and has helped ordinary people achieve success or lead a more positive and fulfilling life.

- Steven Covey is the author of The 7 Habits of Highly Effective People, and his points are regularly quoted in businesses and personal development. These seven habits can be used above and beyond the business realm, applying it to almost anything in life.

- Louise Hay is the author of You Can Heal Your Life and several other motivational and self-improvement books. She promotes self-healing to use the power of our thoughts to enhance our lives.
- Wayne W. Dyer employs the teaching of Tao Te Ching of "Change your thoughts, change your life," which directly influences us to lead and live a more balanced and fulfilling lifestyle. Dyer is the author of The Power of Intention.

Positive thinking and its importance in elevating our social skills and influencing people

Were you ever influenced by someone who looked so unsure of themselves?

When was the last time you purchased something from a salesperson who could not empathize with you?

How many times have you failed at something and someone—a friend, teacher, classmate, parent, or partner—tells you not to give up and focus on the positive?

Sometimes you think it's easier said than done; however, focusing your mind on being and thinking positively is straightforward—it is all about controlling your thoughts. Knowing a positive attitude leads to a fruitful and happy life is already a high motivation to change.

Having a positive outlook on life will enable you to cope more easily with the affairs of everyday life from the moment you wake up until you go to sleep. A positive outlook gives you an optimistic approach and makes you worry less and think fewer negative thoughts. It will enable you to experience the silver lining in the darkest of situations.

A positive mind is a state of mind worth developing because everyone can benefit, and who knows where it will take you?

A positive attitude is noticeable in the following ways:
- Positive thinking
- Constructive thinking
- Creative thinking
- Optimism
- Drive and energy to do things, accomplish goals
- An attitude of happiness

A positive mindset:
- Helps you expect success, as failure is not an option
- Gives the feeling of inspiration in everything you do
- Gives you the strength to keep going and not give up
- Helps you overcome obstacles you face
- Gives you the ability to look at failures, mistakes, and problems as a blessing in disguise
- Keeps you believing in yourself, your abilities, and your talent
- Radiates self-esteem and confidence
- Helps you look for solutions instead of dwelling on problems; you seek opportunities when they come

Positive thinking is a game changer—you can change your whole life if you always look on the bright side of life instead of wallowing in self-pity and allowing yourself to think negatively. Positive thinking is infectious! It not only affects you but each individual around you—people want to be friends with you and hang out with you because of your drive, energy, and positivity, making it so easy to be your friend. You will end up changing the lives of those around you—uplifting them and encouraging them to become the best version of themselves. Positivity is a strong emotion, so if you are positive; you radiate positivity.

Even more benefits of a positive attitude:

- You achieve more of your goals easily.
- You achieve success much rapidly.
- You bring in more happiness into your life and those around you.
- You have more energy to deal with everything life throws at you.
- You have more faith in your abilities and have higher hopes for a brighter future.
- You can inspire and motivate everyone around you.
- You feel you encounter fewer obstacles and difficulties compared to other people.
- You are much more respected and loved by all those around you.
- Life smiles at you.

Chapter 9—Turning Small Talk into Conversation

You can only make small talk for so long. It's a nice ice breaker to forge an initial connection with someone new. However, deeper, more meaningful conversations are what you hope the small talk will develop into if you connect with the right people.

New friendships or business relationships start with small talk before they develop into something more meaningful. But how long should one remain in small talk *before* the conversation develops into something more personal?

That depends entirely on the person you're conversing with. With some people, you connect and click almost instantaneously, while others may need a longer time to warm up before they feel comfortable. Prolonging small talk for too long can eventually feel like a draining experience because it doesn't hold any deeper meaning if it isn't heading in the direction you're hoping for.

You can, however, steer the conversation into the direction you want it to go; the power is entirely in your hands, If you want to turn small talk into real conversation, the following techniques will show you how:

Five Effective Techniques to Turn Small Talk into Conversation

While small talk serves as a great opener, at some point, you want the conversation to go deeper than the surface to see if a genuine connection can be forged between you and this individual you just met.

If you never make small talk, how will you ever gain a friend, close a deal, connect with your co-workers, or even go on a first date? Whether we're shy or we're outgoing, we need social connections because we are social creatures by nature. All you have to do is try going for a week without talking to a single soul, either verbally or through social media to see what a difference it makes in your life and why we need these small talk openers.

#Technique 1: Curiosity Uncovers More – The more curious you are about the person you're talking to, the more you'll want to deepen the conversation beyond just small talk and idle chit-chat. Let your natural curiosity to find out more about the person drive your conversation. Being curious means you're naturally interested and more invested in the conversation. You're thinking about questions that will move the conversation forward beyond just small talk.

Remember to ask open-ended questions and aim for questions that begin with *why* rather than *what*. *Why* questions have a better chance of leading to more meaningful answers, which will help you carry on the conversation longer.

#Technique 2: Tossing Out Different Topics – If you come prepared with a whole range of diverse topics to discuss as part of your small talk strategy, you're already winning before you even begin. By arming yourself with varied topics of discussion, you'll pitch topics back and forth until you finally find a topic both of you can embrace.

A common topic two people can animatedly discuss already opens the door wide for the conversation to develop and progress beyond the small talk banter. A common subject is a thread that unites two people because they can bond over it quickly. This means you don't have to remain in the small talk sphere for long.

#Technique 3: Answer Meaningfully – Remember how a conversation is a two-way street? If you want the conversation to develop into something more, you must play your role beyond just asking the right questions. You must learn to give meaningful answers too. Ideally, questions should bounce back and forth between you and the other person instead of you just bombarding them with one question after another, which is why the way you structure your answers here will matter.

Asking the right questions is a good thing, but returning meaningful answers is even better because people will be curious and interested in knowing more about you the same way you are interested in getting to know more about them. When both sides are interested, a higher chance of building a genuine friendship exists and extends past small talk. When you answer a question, avoid yes and no answers, which are closed-ended and don't encourage further conversational flow. Respond enough to pique the other person's interest so they can't help themselves and will keep asking even more questions. Let the conversation take its course from there.

#Technique 4: Get a Little Personal – Are you comfortable sharing a personal story or experience you think other people might relate to? Remember, this is still a stranger you just met, so don't jump off the deep end and reveal your deepest, darkest secrets and experiences just yet. Instead, start with something you don't mind other people knowing.

Sharing a personal experience won't just increase the other person's interest and curiosity to learn more, but it also potentially leads to them disclosing something personal about themselves. A conversation can quickly go from small talk to something deeper.

This technique is effective in drawing the other person out of their shell and revealing more information about themselves in a way small talk won't. Just be sure not to get *too personal* so you don't risk making anyone uncomfortable.

#Technique 5: Treat Them Like a Friend, not a Stranger You Just Met – One of the biggest roadblocks in small talk is that the person is a stranger you only met five minutes ago. Seeing them as a "stranger" in your mind already sets up barriers for making things awkward and uncomfortable, which makes small talk seem harder than it is. Sure, you may have only met them five minutes ago, but there is no reason you can't see them as a friend or someone you're friendly with.

Avoid using the word stranger in your mind; instead, see them as a friend or pretend you've met them several times before. You don't have to be best friends instantaneously but seeing them from a different perspective will help make the conversational flow less awkward and increase its chances of developing into a more meaningful conversation. When you see the person as a friend, your body language instinctively becomes more open and welcoming as opposed to when you meet a stranger for the first time, and a change in body language will immediately set a different tone for the conversation.

When your body language is friendly, warm, and welcoming, as it would be if you were meeting a friend, the "stranger" will immediately sense this and mirror your body language without even realizing they're doing it. Before you know it, several conversations later, you two could become fast friends.

Key Takeaway Points:

- Curiosity is a natural interest elevator.
- Arm yourself with a range of topics for discussion during the initial small talk phase.

- Pitch ideas and switch topics until you find someone you and the other person can latch on to and connect over.

- Tip: It helps to be present, listen, and pay attention when the other person is talking so you can assess how they respond to various topics and see which one resonates with them more.

- Use common interest topics to help dig deeper into the conversation.

- Give meaningful answers (avoid one-word, close-ended, yes and no responses).

- The right questions and answers will determine the direction in which the conversation is headed.

- Get personal, but not too personal.

- See them as a friend, not a stranger.

Chapter 10—How to Start Great Small Talk with Anyone

The art of winning at small talk is knowing what to say in any social situation. The best thing you can do to prepare is to do your homework beforehand. Prepare a list of conversational starters appropriate to the social setting you're encountering. For example, intellectual and stimulating conversational topics are appropriate during business or client interactions because they are more relatable, whereas fun, light topics and stories are more appropriate for party settings or events where it's about mingling and having fun.

Even if small talk is not your favorite thing in the world, it is unavoidable. So instead of dreading it and doing your best to avoid it, embrace it and start doing what you need to do to *win* at it. Making small talk with strangers you just met doesn't have to be a painful ordeal because you can use some techniques as the ace up your sleeve to make a positive first impression with everyone you meet.

Five Techniques to Start Great Small Talk

Want to start great small talk with just about anyone and hit it off every single time? Here are the five techniques you'll need to pull off:

#Technique 1: Don't Panic – If small talk makes you nervous already, then lulls and awkward pauses in conversation certainly won't help. Panicking, though, isn't of much help to you either. Sometimes silence is ok, especially when you or the other person need a minute or two to think about what you will say next. Panicking and fumbling for something to say could cause you to say something inappropriate.

Instead, use those short pauses to your advantage by taking a quick moment to process your thoughts as you look for the next topic of conversation. Also, assess how the conversation is going. Is the other person interested? Do they look bored? Do they look like they're not in the mood for small talk? Get a good read of their body language by being observant because it'll give you a good idea about how you should proceed. Don't try to force conversation because it will just be a strain on both of you.

#Technique 2: Make Yourself Approachable – Start off on the right foot immediately by doing this one, simple thing—make yourself approachable. You don't even have to do much except keep an open body language and smile with sincerity. Keeping an open body language here means relax, don't slouch and appear uncomfortable, don't cross your arms in front of you (it signals you're closed off to other people), look around interestedly and smile openly with anyone you make eye contact with.

A smile is the best body language ice-breaking weapon everyone possesses at their disposal, and it lights up your face entirely. If the other person is feeling ill at ease, they will immediately relax when they see how warm and friendly you appear to be; conversations are more inclined to start on a positive note. When they approach you and if you're meeting them for the first time, greet them warmly and show genuine interest. If you've met them before, greet them again in a friendly manner and greet them by name; this lets them know you're pleased to be talking to them.

#Technique 3: Don't Psyche Yourself Out Negatively – Self-fulfilling prophecy is a real thing. It's probably happened to you a couple of times, and we don't generally realize our own thoughts have made it so. Thoughts are so powerful—the more intensely we focus on them, the more likely they are to become a reality. If you want to win at small talk, you must stop psyching yourself out negatively.

Don't approach small talk sessions with an attitude of *why am I doing this* or *I hate small talk; I'm never any good at it,* or *I'm always awful at small talk; this won't go well.* If you keep approaching small talk with that mindset, it never will go well. Instead, think of it as something you need because it will benefit you and it's for your own good. Each relationship you build along the way could open a range of possibilities and opportunities you might have otherwise missed out on.

Look forward to small talk sessions and see them as a door leading to something new.

#Technique 4: Make it Universal – One key to approaching small talk with a stranger and winning is to keep the topics of conversation general or universal. Unless you've already met a few times, stick to universal topics everyone can relate to.

General topics such as entertainment, movies, sports, the weather, or current news are generally considered safe enough as small talk starters for strangers. Don't surprise the person you're talking to with a strange or random topic, which will just leave them staring in blank confusion at you. Remember, small talk could be just as uncomfortable for them in the beginning as it is for you, so it is up to you to take control of the situation by setting the right tone for the conversation right from the beginning. Small talk is meant to be light-hearted and informal, so avoid starting with something deep and heavy right from the beginning; save that for people you know personally.

Keep some general or universal topics on hand before heading to any social setting. Not only will you be better prepared to kick off conversations on the right note, but you'll feel a lot less anxious and stressed because you're already prepared beforehand. A little preparation can go a long way.

#Technique 5: The No Phone Policy – Now, this technique might be hard to stomach, especially for those addicted to checking your mobiles every couple of minutes, but you must do it. Put. Down. That. Phone. Now.

By default, our first instinct these days is to immediately reach for our mobile phones whenever we're uncomfortable, by ourselves, or feeling awkward—just so we look busy like we've got something to do. Whipping out your mobile phone during small talk conversations can spell disaster and be an immediate conversation killer. You're signaling to the other person you're completely disinterested and your phone is more interesting than them or anything they have to say.

Whenever you're in a social setting, and you have found no one to talk to just yet, squash the instinct to pull out your phone and scroll through it. Nobody will approach you if you're preoccupied with your phone. The minute you pay more attention to your phone than to the people around you, it kills and sabotages any possible small talk opportunity you might have had. Would you approach someone constantly on their phone all the time? Put your phone down; the social media alerts and updates can wait. Be more interested in your surroundings and the people around you.

<u>**Key Takeaway Points:**</u>

- Don't panic.
- Read the other person's body language during pauses in conversation.
- Make yourself approachable.

- Use pauses in conversation to your advantage by mentally assessing how it's going.

- Smile.

- Make the person you're talking to feel as comfortable as possible.

- Greet them warmly.

- Don't psyche yourself out negatively.

- Approach small talk with a positive attitude.

- Stick to the general topics.

- Put your phone away; it's a conversation killer.

Chapter 11—The Five-Step Guide to General Small Talk

By now, you're already well-prepared to have better small talk conversations with just about anyone you meet. No longer will you have to stand awkwardly in a room feeling uncomfortable as you count the minutes ticking by or feel nervous with the strangers you encounter, hoping to just make it through without feeling too uncomfortable.

There's small talk, and then there's *effective* small talk, and you want to aim to achieve the latter. Love it or hate it, small talk isn't going away anytime soon, and by now, we've established this is a lifelong skill you could immensely benefit from if you know what you're doing and do it right.

In this chapter, we'll explore the five remaining techniques out of your thirty-one-technique process, and these five will focus on how to get the best results out from general small talk.

How to Make the Best Out of General Small Talk

#Technique 1: Focus on Shared Interests – As you banter during your small talk sessions, you'll eventually (hopefully) land on a topic of common interest between you and the person you're conversing with. This won't happen for everyone though, because you just won't be on the same wavelength with some people no matter how hard you try. Don't worry; this is normal. With billions of people in the world, you're bound to encounter this occasionally.

When you land on a topic of common interest during your small talk sessions, focus on that because it is much easier to connect and deepen the connection when you're both animatedly bonding over something you're interested in. It is definitely a lot more personal than talking about the weather. Start your small talk sessions with the aim of finding a common or shared interest, and begin with a purpose in mind. This will help you stay focused instead of aimlessly just winging it.

#Technique 2: Keep It Positive – People are put off by negativity. Wouldn't you be? Nobody wants to engage in small talk with someone who is constantly complaining about everything. No one wants to be around an aura of negativity. If you wouldn't like being around someone like that, don't be guilty of doing the same thing.

If you're engaging in small talk with someone, keep it positive. If all you can do is complain and whine, you will put people off, and they'll quickly lose interest in prolonging the conversation. If you're having a bad day, need to blow off a little steam, and your head isn't in the right place, it is best not to engage in small talk with anyone. Small talk is not the time to vent your feelings. If you are having an off day but you know you must engage in some important small talk later, find a way to relax and calm your nerves, clear your mind, and lift your spirits again. Always keep it positive because it is important to be friendly, upbeat, and cheerful in conversations so they leave with a good first impression of you.

#Technique 3: Pause Between Sentences – Don't feel pressured to let out a stream of verbiage because you're afraid awkward silences may follow. Firing off one topic after another and question after question could make the other person uncomfortable. Plus, you're not giving the other person a chance to get a word in edgewise.

During small talk, it is important to be considerate of the other person's feelings because it isn't just about you. Yes, you may be keen to engage in small talk, but you need to keep in mind the other person may not be feeling the same way. Maybe they're just not up for it then or they're distracted. Either way, give them some space and room to breathe, give them a chance to interject their opinions or share their thoughts, and, more importantly, give them a chance to leave the conversation if they want to. There's no point forcing someone to engage in small talk if they're just not up for it at the moment.

#Technique 4: Let Your Conversation Partner Do the Teaching – Small talk isn't just a great way to make a new connection; it is also a great opportunity to learn something new. Some people love sharing what they know, especially if they feel like they could teach something in the process. If you are not familiar with a topic your conversation partner wants to talk about, don't be afraid to admit it. You will be surprised at just how eager they are to teach you about it most of the time.

We discussed earlier how people love to talk about themselves. They want to know people just like you who take a keen interest in them and what they have to say. Besides, it gives you a chance to ask insightful questions, too, which opens the door for the conversation to develop into something more meaningful.

#Technique 5: Practice Makes Perfect – Small talk shouldn't be just something you fall back on when it could be beneficial for you. You shouldn't only try to engage in small talk when it's necessary, such as during important events, functions, or client meetings. If you only attempt to engage in small talk during those moments, it will take you a while to improve your skills until you've had enough practice.

Instead, make it a point to practice small talk with everyone you meet. It could be the doorman at your apartment, the person waiting for you at the bus stop, someone you're riding the elevator with, or even the person next to you as you're queueing for your morning cup of coffee. Plenty of opportunities exist to make small talk with just about everyone, even the little encounters we have on a daily basis. These moments are perfect opportunities to practice your small talk skills, and with each encounter, you will learn how to improve and what you could do better. That way, when it's time for those big events, you can ace it like a pro because you've already had plenty of practice.

Key Takeaway Points:

- Begin small talk sessions with a goal and a purpose in mind to help you stay focused.

- When trying to bond with the other person, try to find a common or shared interest to make it easier.

- When you find a shared interest, focus on it to help you deepen your personal connection.

- Keep it positive.

- Do not complain or emit negative emotions during your small talk sessions; you will just put the other person off.

- Don't fire off questions one after another.

- It is okay to pause between sentences to give the other person a chance to talk.

- See small talk as an opportunity to learn something new.

- Ask insightful questions.

- Practice small talk as often as you can. The more you practice, the better your skills will be.

Chapter 12—Understanding Body Language

Body language is one of the many ways we humans communicate. Most people pay attention to words and actions, but rarely body language. What we say can sometimes be different from our body language. We may sound happy, but our body language says otherwise, and according to experts, our body language makes up half of the way we communicate.

Learning to read body language effectively can help us understand what someone is trying to say, if they are comfortable with the choices made, and if they are genuine about it. We also learn to communicate our messages effectively when we learn to read body language. It goes beyond just what words can say.

How common is body language in communication?

Believe it or not, body language makes up 55 percent of our daily communication. However, analyzing nonverbal cues isn't focused on just the broad strokes. These gestures indicate various things, and it depends entirely on context. Nonverbal cues are crucial when trying to read someone because, in many ways, you can detect if someone is lying or if they are enjoying a date or how they are as a person when they come in for a job interview. It is about reading between the lines to interpret body language accurately so you know if the person's words convey how they genuinely feel.

Unfortunately, we humans are more inclined to lie than tell the truth for plenty of reasons, such as avoiding conflict, trying to impress someone, and so on. Sometimes we end up lying more than once in a short span of time, and while they may necessarily not be big lies, we end up willingly partaking in deception because we would rather hear a sweet lie than the bitter truth. But body language is not as deceptive as words—the human body is a terrible liar.

What Is Body Language?

Body language is our body's physical, non-verbal communication approach sometimes in-sync with the words coming out of our mouth. Body language can be anything from a stance, an eye-glance, a quick facial expression, and even biting our lip.

You may have seen how some people speak animatedly and mostly use their hands to convey or emphasize their words. Plenty of hand talkers keep their hands in constant motion to convey their point, emphasize information, or just to keep the conversation moving along.

This gesture and many other forms of body language often speak volumes. Observe a person's body language in the following scenarios:

a) When they speak:

- Do they have slumped shoulders? Is their back rounded with their head hanging down? This could indicate they are either shy or sad.

b) When you see a person walking into a room to address a team or a company:

- Do they have a firm walk? Is their chest puffed out, shoulders raised? Do they have their head at eye level or held high? This can be interpreted as arrogance or confidence.

c) When you need to talk to someone:

- Do they have their arms folded across their chest? Are their legs crossed? Are they glancing around or sighing? This could be understood as an unfriendly stance, or they are not open to what you have to say; they are defensive or standoffish.

It is truly fascinating how much we can perceive from body language. You can not only use body language to judge a person's mood or attitude, but you can also make and create better relationships simply by observing them. These non-verbal communication gateways help create a deeper sense of bonding.

Body Language Basics

Your main goal in reading body language is to determine if a person is comfortable. Once you have established this, the next thing is to process the context and look at other cues. This is easier said than done, so we will go into the specifics in the following chapters. Here are some common denominators for positive body language:

- Moving or leaning closer to you
- Feeling at ease
- Relaxed, uncrossed limbs
- Long periods of eye contact
- Looking down and away out of shyness
- Genuine smiles

Here are some common denominators for negative body language:

- Moving or leaning away from you
- The feeling of unease
- Crossed arms or legs

- Looking away to the side

- Feet pointed away from you, or toward and exit

- Rubbing/scratching their nose, eyes, or the back of their neck

One body cue can mean plenty of different things. While crossed arms can be construed as negative body language, it can also suggest the person is feeling cold, uncomfortable, or frustrated or closed off, or even they are more comfortable sitting that way. When reading someone, it is crucial to pay attention to several behavioral cues because looking at one can be misleading. You need to look deeper to understand what is going on, and this means focusing on cues and the context.

Here are some common body language categories:

Body Language Categories

Body language can be broken down into general categories.

1. Aggressive – This indicates threatening body language.

2. Attentiveness – This shows you are interested and engaged.

3. Bored – This is the opposite of attentiveness, and it is usually represented by the lack of eye contact and constant yawning.

4. Closed – This is when someone shuts you off and is often shown with crossed arms and standing far away.

5. Deceptiveness – This is usually portrayed when a person wants to get away with a lie and displays nervous behavior and acts guilty and worried.

6. Defensiveness – This person can look like they are protecting or withholding information.

7. Dominant – This body language is used when someone wants to be in command, and they usually stand tall, with their chest puffed out.

8. Emotional – When a person is emotional, they are heavily influenced by their current feelings and usually have changing moods.

9. Evaluation – A person, portrays a sense of evaluation when making a decision or even hesitating to make a choice.

10. Greeting – This happens when two people first come into contact.

11. Open – This body language is friendly and welcoming.

12. Ready – This tells people you are open, willing, and prepared.

13. Content and relaxed – This can be portrayed by a calm, happy, and restful demeanor.

14. Passionate – This is often a romantic body language expressing attraction and flirtation.

15. Submissive – This shows off the relenting side.

These body languages are usually commonly communicated through a combination of postures and poses not just one. Again, many body positions have entirely different meanings depending on the context, the situation, and the cultural background. Take, for example, the pose of crossing your arms—in a meeting situation, this can be construed as simply being serious and focused.

It is crucial to take context into consideration, and if you want to learn how to analyze people, then develop a heightened sense of awareness of how your body acts and what it is saying when you talk to the people around you. Keeping these tips in mind will help increase your communication and comprehension skills, thus opening a more effective line of communication with your team, your partner, children, and friends.

Chapter 14—Becoming a Better Communicator

In this chapter, we explore practical exercises you can cultivate and practice to help you communicate better and develop better social skills. In communicating, there are always two sides of a story, and both are essential to ensure the message comes across as intended by both the giver and receiver. You should be a good talker and a good listener. Nobody likes it if all you do is talk or just talk about yourself without asking the other person their thoughts, ideas, and concerns.

1. The first rule: learn to listen

Learning to listen is a crucial element in a successful conversation. As mentioned above, nobody likes it if all you do is talk without asking what is going on in their life. A successful conversation means both parties are active participants, both parties talk and listen, and the message communicated has been understood in the same context. When communicating, we become both the talker and the listener, just at two different times. Here is how you can master both:

When you are doing the talking

- Get your thinking straight – Muddled thinking is the most common source of confusing messages. Most of the time, when we have an idea, we haven't thought it through or we have plenty to say but do not know how to convey it properly. When this happens, we come across as ill-prepared, our ideas and thoughts are not conveyed properly, and we end up confusing everyone. To prevent this, the first rule is to think before you say anything. In this way, you can better articulate your ideas and organize your thoughts, thus conveying a clear and concise message.

- Say what you mean – Quit using confusing jargon and big words. Tell someone exactly what you mean when you communicate. You will be surprised how a simple sentence can convey your message more beautifully than hard-to-understand, long sentences.

- Get to the point – When you do not get to the point, you're not only wasting the other person's time but yours as well. If you want to communicate effectively, do not beat around the bush but instead get to the point. Make your objectives and the purpose of the conversation clear. If you want something, ask for it. If you need help, ask. If you want something to be explained, seek help.

- Be concise – By not getting to the point, being long-winded, and stretching the conversation, you are only creating confusion. The more words used, the greater the confusion. Speak plainly using short and familiar words.

- Be authentic – To ensure clarity of your message and goals, be authentic in presenting your message. Use your own personality and just be you when you speak. Take into context the situation you are in. For example, if you are doing a presentation for a client, be polite and confident but not pompous and stuck up. Let the real you shine because, in this way, you will be more convincing and comfortable when you convey your thoughts and ideas.

- Stop to look and listen – Looking and listening are crucial in conversations. We all know how images can paint a thousand words, so when speaking, you can also help the receiver of your message visualize your content by giving examples or even using facial expressions and gestures. Listening to social cues happening around you helps you convey a message and helps the listener understand what you are saying.

When you are doing the listening

- Listen with care and thought – Like speaking and writing, listening also requires genuine attention and interest. You will not learn much if you do not actively listen and the rate of remembering anything will not be high either. According to research, we retain only 25 percent of what we hear; therefore, if you want to increase your retention rate and your understanding of something, you need to increase how effectively you listen.

-

- Use your eyes – The eyes are the windows to our soul, and if you listen only with your ears, you are missing out on understanding the message. To become a good and active listener, you also need to activate your eyes to look at what the speaker is saying. This not only enhances the listening, but it also shows or tells the speaker you are genuinely interested in what is being said. Our face is a communication medium, and we use it to learn to read messages both verbal and non-verbal. The face can so say many things, so it is imperative to convey our attention through non-verbal cues.

- Make things easy

- People who are not good listeners find that few people come to them with or for useful information. People who are good listeners, on the other hand, are approachable and make it easy for people to understand them simply because they listen and make it clear if they are interested or not.

2. Three exercises to do every day to improve your language skills

Part of improving your language skills is practicing good habits. These habits and practices are extremely good for you because they help you reach your goals. As you have realized by now, to have good language skills, you need to practice. The issue most of us face isn't so much about starting a new goal—it is more to do with sustaining motivation to attain a long-term goal.

How do you change your habits? Here are some ways to practice change and cultivate good habits:

Breaking bad habits

1. Replace a bad habit with a positive one. If you want to quit smoking, try running. If you want to limit playing computer games, start reading magazines and comics.

2. Take on a weekly challenge or, better yet, a thirty-day challenge. It is said to cultivate a habit or a new way of life, you need to practice it for at least twenty-one days.

3. Commit and give it 100 percent. If you have a new challenge, put yourself into it entirely and tell someone close to you so they can motivate you and remind you of your goals whenever you lack motivation.

4. Create a blog or post things on Instagram to maintain a sense of responsibility and keep track of your performance and progress. This helps you stay motivated.

5. Reward yourself. Setting up rewards at the end of the week helps you stay on track and stay motivated.

6. Stay positive. Having a positive mental attitude is the most critical aspect. One way to stay positive is to surround yourself with positive people and those with the same mindset and goals as you.

7. Invest thirty minutes or an hour of your time every day toward reaching your goal. So if your goal is speed reading, then practice every day until you reach your goal.

Managing stress to ensure a positive and healthy mind and body

1. Practicing breathing and stretching exercises for at least ten minutes a day can do wonders for your mind and body. Do this daily either in the morning or before bed.

2. Listen to calming music when you wake up in the morning.

3. Take your dog for a walk in the park. A walk in the park or outdoors can do so much for your emotional and mental well-being.

4. Detach yourself from anything causing your stress. If it is a job or project, take a day or two away from it so you can recover. If it is an argument, give yourself a five-minute break. You will be surprised at how much this helps.

5. Sniff essential oils; geranium and lavender have soothing effects on the body.

6. Painting or coloring is also a great way to destress and rejuvenate, especially on weekdays after work.

7. Have long baths whenever you feel stressed. Better yet, light candles or have your essential oils during this *me* time.

8. If you are facing a stressful time at work, chew a piece of gum or squeeze a stress ball.

9. Dress up well. Dressing up for anything elevates your mood, so do it even if it is for a job you hate.

10. Retail therapy is also another way to reduce stress levels.

11. Reading spiritual texts or meditating is also another way to reduce stress in your life.

12. Take a walk in the woods. Nature is always good therapy.

13. Perform an act of kindness. You will be surprised by how much helping other people will help with your inner conscious and well-being.

14. Eat your favorite foods. If your goal is to reduce weight, then indulge in healthier alternatives such as vegan ice cream and gluten-free brownies. You always have options. Besides, treating yourself occasionally is the key to staying happy and on track.

Being more mindful

1. Stop and smell the fresh air. Most of the time, we are always in a rush, and we rarely see our surroundings or the little things our family and friends do to improve our lives. So take life one step at a time occasionally. Be mindful of the people closest to you.

2. Let go of worry and regret. The past is there to teach you, and you learn from it, but you need to move on.

3. Focus on immediate sensations such as kissing your husband or wife when you get home after a long day, drinking a cup of hot chocolate on a cold night, or finally getting in your bed to sleep.

Creating Positive Social Goals

1. Social goals are important because they help you attain other goals in your life.

2. Make a conscious effort to smile at the people you meet.

3. Say good morning to your colleagues.

4. Laugh as much as you can and don't take yourself too seriously. Laughter is bonding.

5. Invest in personal hygiene and new clothes. Showering and grooming help you stay alert and focused and ready for challenges the day has for you.

6. Do not complain or gossip, and let go of gripes. Remove yourself from negative situations.

7. Stretch as much as you can—even at work. Rolling your shoulders, stretching your leg, and other little exercises help you open up and breathe better.

3. Tips and tricks to create empathy in real life (not as shown to us in the movies)

Empathy is the ability to recognize how people feel in a certain scenario. Having this ability is crucial to success both in your career and in your life. The more you can decipher the feelings of others, the better you can manage your thoughts and approaches toward them. Empathetic people are excellent at:

• Recognizing, anticipating, and meeting a person's needs

• Developing the needs of other people and bolstering their individual abilities

• Taking advantage of diversity by cultivating opportunities among different people

• Developing political awareness by understanding the current emotional state of people and fostering powerful relationships

• Focusing on identifying feelings and wants of other people

Developing good interpersonal skills is imperative as well if you want a successful life and a successful career. In our world today, when plenty of things are digitized, social skills seem to be an afterthought. People skills are more relevant and sought-after than before since now you also need a high EQ to understand, negotiate, and empathize with others, especially if you interact with different people on a daily basis. Among the most useful skills are:

- Influence to effectively wield persuasive tactics

- Communication to send clear and concise messages

- Leadership to inspire and guide people and groups

- Change catalyst in kick-starting and managing change

- Managing conflicting situations, which include the ability to negotiate, understand, and resolve disagreements

- Bonding and nurturing meaningful and instrumental relationships

- Teamwork, cooperation, and collaboration in meeting shared goals

- Creating a synergetic group to work toward collective goals

Chapter 15—Developing Emotional Intelligence

Emotional intelligence is a highly valuable asset. It is the ability to manage and identify which emotions belong to you and which emotions belong to others. Emotional intelligence encompasses three skills, which are:

1. Emotional awareness

2. The ability to capitalize emotions and use them on certain tasks, such as problem-solving and thinking

3. The ability to manage emotions, which involves regulating personal emotions, cheering people up, or calming them down

The term Emotional Intelligence, often referred to as EQ or EI, was coined by researchers Peter Salovey and John Mayer and later popularized by Dan Goleman in his book of the same name in 1996.

With emotional intelligence, you can:

- Recognize, understand, and manage your own personal emotions

•Recognize, understand, and influence other people's emotions

Being aware of these abilities means knowing emotions can drive our behavior and impact those around us, either positively or negatively. It also means we can manage these emotions—both our own and others'—especially at pressuring and stressful times.

The Five Categories of Emotional Intelligence (EQ)

Regarding Emotional Intelligence, five categories exist.

1. Self-awareness

Self-awareness means having the ability to recognize an emotion as and when it occurs, and it is the key to your EQ. To develop self-awareness, a person needs to tune into their own feelings, evaluating them and subsequently managing them.

For self-awareness, the important elements are:

•Recognizing our own emotions and its effects

•Having a level of confidence and sureness of your capabilities and your self-worth

2. Self-regulation.

When we experience emotions, we often have little control over our actions at first. One thing we can control, however, is how long these emotions last. To control how long certain emotions last, especially negative ones, certain methods are used to lessen the effects of emotions such as anxiety, anger, and even depression. These methods include reinventing a scenario in a positive manner, such as taking a long walk, saying a prayer, and even meditating.

Self-regulation includes:

•Innovation, which means open to new ideas

•Adaptability to handle change and be flexible

•Trustworthiness, referring to the ability to keep standards of integrity and honesty

•Taking responsibility, conscientiousness of our own actions

•Self-control to prevent disruptive impulses

3. Motivation

Having motivation helps us accomplish our tasks and goals and maintain an air of positivity. With practice and effort, we can all program our minds to be more positive, although as human beings, it is also good to be negative at times. Negative thoughts are not necessarily bad, but they should be kept in check, as they cause more harm than good. Whenever you have negative feelings, you choose the positive aspects of the situation, the silver lining, which will help you be more focused on solving the problem.

Motivation consists of:

•Having a sense of achievement drive to constantly strive to improve and meet a level of excellence

•Having the commitment to align your individual, group, or organizational goals

•Having the initiative to act on available opportunities

•Having the optimism to pursue your goals persistently and objectively, despite the setbacks and obstacles

Which element is more important—High IQ or High EQ?

The first question to ask is, what is a success to you? Is it having loads of money? Is it about having a successful career? Is it about having a family? How well you do in life depends not only on emotional intelligence but also intelligence, luck, and passion. EQ alone is not enough, and neither is IQ alone enough.

Psychologies agree the elements of success depend on having an IQ count at roughly 10 percent being the minimum and 25 percent at its best. The other elements of success depend on everything else, which includes EQ.

It's just like exercise. Working out five days a week alone is not enough. Motivation to follow a balanced diet and work out regularly, and making exercise a lifestyle rather than an option, are among the traits to achieve a successful and healthy body weight.

What can you do to increase your emotional intelligence?

1. Observe your feelings

One of the first things we lose touch with is our emotions, especially when we focus all our energy on worrying about what to do next and what we can do better. Instead of focusing on our emotions, we instead often ignore them. Things become worse when we suppress our emotions instead of dealing with them. When we keep covering up our emotions, we tend to lose control of them, which is not a good thing.

When we experience an emotional reaction toward something, it is always because we have unresolved issues. The next time you feel a negative emotion taking up space in your mind and heart, take a five-minute breather, calm down, and think about what you are experiencing and the possible reasons for these emotions. Write things down and try to identify your triggers and how you can deal with them.

2. Practice responding, not reacting

When we react, often we do it unconsciously to relieve the emotions we are experiencing or express what is going through our mind. When we respond consciously, we are more adept at paying attention to our own feelings and become better at deciding how we will react to these emotions and our feelings. As we become more aware of our emotional triggers, we become more aware of how to adapt, how to respond, and how to behave.

For instance, if you know you get angry easily and have a habit of throwing a temper, especially when things get stressful, relive this moment when you are alone. Think about how you could react the next time to prevent yourself from experiencing the same trigger.

Speak to your colleagues and tell them you need a time-out to gather your thoughts. If you must, leave the room for some fresh air. Count to ten even. Once you have calmed down a little, you will be better at dealing with the issues that made you angry in the first place.

4. Stay humble all the time.

Staying humble enables you to form better and more meaningful relationships. When you presume you are better than other people, it becomes harder to see your own faults, and you will easily get emotional over things that do not meet your expectations or needs. To prevent this, look at things from a different perspective or put yourself in the person's shoes and understand how they feel or think about a certain situation. Doing so makes you more prone to understanding people's thoughts and feelings. You will also learn a thing or two about how to deal with similar situations. Being humble is knowing you are not any better than anyone else and wise enough to know you are special in your own way.

Creating Emotional Balance and Enhancing Self-Esteem

Emotional balance is the ability to maintain equilibrium and flexibility between the mind and body when we face changes or challenges. So how we do create emotional balance? Here are some ways:

1. Accept your emotions

Many of our mental, emotional, and physical problems stem from our inability to express ourselves emotionally. When we are emotionally distraught, we smother it in the comforts of eating, sleeping, sweating it out, or sucking it up; it is swept under a rug, we bury it, project it elsewhere, or meditate hoping to suppress our emotions instead of actually dealing with it and accepting it. The key here is to allow ourselves unconditional permission to feel—to cry when we want to, to feel anger when we are angry, sadness when we grieve, and so on. Let your guard down either when you are alone or with someone you trust and just focus on the feeling and situation.

Experience and immerse yourself in this feeling so you can comprehend better why it hurts and what you will do to remedy the situation once you've accepted and acknowledged these feelings.

2. Express yourself

Expressing yourself is important and can be done in many ways. Usually, when we experience a feeling, we react by crying, shouting, or throwing things. But to manage our emotions properly, we can also express ourselves in more positive ways. Some people like reading, as it provides an escape into a different world. Some people express themselves through art or music. Whatever you do, make sure you stay connected to discover more about yourself, your identity, and the person you want to become.

3. Don't hide your feelings

Sometimes, it is easy to hide our feelings and not think about them, especially painful and scary memorics. But as we all know, hiding your memories and feelings will only make things worse for you. While it is hard to address your fears and sadness, rage and anger, once you actually dive into it, you will find it easier to face your fears, and, eventually, the choppy waters will become calmer.

Be accepting your past and dealing with it in a more emotional state, you ultimately will lead a harmonious life. Always allow yourself to feel because your reactions to these different feelings are more stable than an overreaction.

4. See the world in a positive light

It is easier said than done, we know. The world is full of hatred, sadness, grief, war, crime, and unfairness—it is a threat to our emotional health. You tend to develop low self-esteem and start asking yourself if you are worth it, if you can get through it, if you are doing things right, and all these thoughts steer you toward making more mistakes and missteps. Rather than having emotional self-doubt, take action to develop a prerogative of seeing the world in a more positive light.

Do not feel responsible when bad things happen that you didn't cause. Have compassion on yourself and practice mindfulness. Accept that occasional lapses and failures are just part of being human.

5. Get a grip on your mind

The way we think causes us emotional distress—this probably is not news to you. We all have a tendency to overthink, and these thoughts do not serve you or give you any positivity; they just set you up for emotional distress. So get a grip on your mind—do not let it wander too much, especially when you start overthinking.

6. Practice yoga and mindfulness

Doing yoga on a daily basis helps your mental health by increasing your confidence in your abilities; it also helps you make better definitive decisions.

You also learn not to be so self-criticizing. Yoga can help get rid of negative energy within you and help you work your way toward mental clarity and vital energy. Also, the breathing practiced in yoga helps you relax better and makes you calmer, especially if your mind is racing, and it also helps you refine your feelings.

Breathing correctly helps you get rid of stress and anxiety as well.

Chapter 16—Breaking Mental Barriers—an Introvert's Guide

In chapter 4, we discussed various personality tests and how they beneficial to figure out who you are as a person and make sense of how you react to certain things, your perception, and your preferences.

We also discussed how we should not confine or define ourselves based on the traits or descriptions of the test results.

This is where breaking down our mental barriers is so important—especially for introverts.

Introverts are slightly misunderstood. They like spending time on their own, but alone time isn't the only thing they enjoy. Introverts do enjoy socializing with people they know and are familiar with. Company and conversation with people they are close to is preferable to a night of partying and meeting so many new people.

The challenge with introverts is initiating a conversation. They don't dislike the presence of people and conversation. Extroverts are the same —while they do love socializing and interacting with people, they, too, need some alone to re-energize.

For introverts, trouble usually ensues when you find yourself in a conversation with someone you don't know well, and then what do you do? Here you are talking beautifully with three people where you know one person well but not the other two. The person you know well leaves the conversation, and you're left standing there awkwardly, trying to figure out what to say.

How do you speak with someone you don't know? What topics can you talk about? How can you network with someone without knowing what to say?

Most importantly, how will you convince them to join your cause, donate to your charity, give you a job, or invest in your start-up when you're having a hard time even striking a conversation with them?

Try F.O.R.D.

If you are shy and do not know what to say to someone you do not know well, here are some topics you can talk about even if you are not shy, but you don't know where to begin.

It starts with F.O.R.D.—Family, Occupation, Recreation, and Dreams.

- Talking about your family

  Talking about family is a safe conversation topic—everyone has a family, in some form or another. Ask your conversation partner questions like where their family is from or if they have any siblings. The answers usually enable you to come up with more questions. "Oh, you have four siblings? Me too. How many girls, how many boys?" Or "Your family is from Michigan? I have a cousin who lives there. I just love the food there." You can also ask if they are married or single and what their spouse or partner does for a living. Naturally, these questions also lead to whether they have children. If you have kids of your own, the topic of conversation here is endless. You can talk about where your kids go to school, what they are like, how old they are, and so on.

•Talking about your job

"What do you do for a living?" is a good way to ask about their job. Some may say what they are currently doing; some may say they are in between jobs. Whatever the answer is, you can definitely move the conversation along by asking how long they have been in their job, what a day on the job look like, their least favorite aspect of the job, their most favorite part, and how they began. You will be surprised how much you can talk about just by asking someone about their career, and you might just find something you both can click on.

•Recreation or hobbies

"What do you do in your free time?" usually comes after asking someone about their jobs and careers. For instance, if your conversation partner isn't open to talking about their jobs because they were recently laid off or something, you can move the conversation along to what they enjoy as a hobby. Ask them about the books they'd like to read or even better—what series they are watching on Netflix. Find out if they have been learning anything new lately, whether it is a new language, a new form of art, or even self-defense. You might just end up gaining a new friend who shares the same interests as you. You can also talk about travel plans for the year, the places they have been to, or even what they did during the weekend.

•Ask them about their dreams

This may seem like a weird conversation topic, but once you ask them straightforward questions about their family and about their job, asking them about their dream job would be surprising but not unconventional. Your conversation partner might find this to be totally out of the blue and actually be interested in pursuing the conversation with you longer than expected. Also, this surprising question might also make them more comfortable talking with you, cutting the awkwardness. Ask them about their dream vacation or what's on their bucket list or even their dream house.

It's about forming close relationships.

While you would rather go home to a hot cup of cocoa and read books about business growth, deep down, you know networking your way through the right people will help further your cause. Networking is tricky and daunting but save yourself from all the anxiety and just remember this:

You want to create meaningful and close relationships with a select few whom you know you can count on. You want to know which contact would work best for which situation, not have thousands of people in your network with no clue who to call, and who would be available and ready to help or joint venture with you.

Just as you have a close group of friends you can count on and have meaningful friendships with, you need the same with your networking contacts.

Have a good pool of ten to fifteen people on your list who can directly and positively advocate your business. From then on, you can continue networking and just add one or two more to the pool. Keeping your business contacts to a number you can count on your fingers is a lot better than having a whole Rolodex of people you can't count on when the time comes.

Bottom Line

You do not need to memorize all the F.O.R.D. questions, nor do you need to write them on your arm in case of an emergency socializing moment. You just need to remember the formula and memorize three to four questions you like best and are comfortable discussing. Remember, this is as much for you as it is for them.

Chapter 17—Developing Your Persuasion Skills

Having good persuasion skills is an essential element in the social process and leads to commitment toward your networking goals. Part of networking is convincing the people we meet who have different needs, values, visions, goals, and networking agendas.

When we are part of an organization, a company, or even running our own business, we need to persuade the people we encounter who play an integral part in ensuring our goals are met. We need to persuade our bosses our idea solves the problem. We need to convince our peers to be part of the idea to get it to work. We need to persuade our direct line managers, partners, superiors, clients, and vendors to be part of our agenda, to be part of our goals, to invest in our idea, to buy our product, or to commit to our service.

Influencing people is a common playground if you are part of the business or work space. If we do not have the art of persuasion, we can never make our vision materialize.

Influence

Influence is a word taken from the Latin word *influere,* which means to flow into. Influence means the capacity of someone to affect, to transform, and to shape and form the opinions, behaviors, or actions of other people with no formal authority over them. The art of persuasion and influencing is soft, and it is a form of personal power; it is not positional power. It allows people, especially leaders, to get things done and achieve an organizational agenda with no coercion.

Believe it or not, we learn to influence in childhood. It happens in families, between parent and child, among friends, in the workplace, in communities, and, generally, toward the larger society. Also, on average, a person influences about fifty to one hundred people a day. Influencing is one of the four critical leadership components important for a business owner, entrepreneur, or someone who wants to pursue greater career goals and further their organizational goals.

What happens when you successfully influence people?

Influencing people is an essential skill, especially when you are networking. The position of the person doing the networking—in this case, you—is to sell your idea or the ideas of those you represent. When you successfully influence someone, you gain their commitment and compliance, but if things go wrong, you meet with some resistance.

• Commitment:

Those who develop good influencing skills can achieve their goals more effectively. When you successfully influence people, you gain their commitment toward your cause, which also means voluntary support. You also do not need to monitor them or follow up on them as frequently because they are invested in your idea or cause and are actively participating in its progress, showcasing a higher sustained effort over time. You both have a better focus on the outcomes of your partnership and have developed improved interpersonal relationships.

- **Compliance:**

Influencing, on a moderate level, develops compliance. This happens if the influencing is less effective and people just comply with it, but their attitudes or mindsets do not change. Compliance is not necessarily a bad thing because it can lead to higher productivity. It works for well-defined ideas or goals that do not require a high sense of engagement, creativity, or decision-making from the other party.

- **Resistance:**

Poor influencing leads to resistance either by sabotaging or by obstructing. This happens when a person asks a higher authority to overrule your ideas, goals, or project, or they attempt to persuade you to renounce your idea. They also look for excuses not to participate or even pretend to comply.

How do you effectively influence people?

This chapter will not be complete if we do not talk about *how* to effectively and efficiently influence people. To do this, we look at the Head, Heart, and Hands. Each of these components needs to work seamlessly to achieve the desired effect. You can use different ways to influence behaviors and the opinions of people. You can use facts and logic, appeals to their beliefs and values, or even supporting their ideas and goals.

When networking, you can use the tactics of logical, emotional, and cooperative. They do not harm the existing relationship at all, so don't worry.

1. **The Head:** This is the *Logical* tactic of influencing where you address people or present your case in a rational or intellectual way. Facts and figures, statistics, and logic make up most of the arguments and information. These facts and figures are presented in the best interest of the organization, the team, or the person.

2. **The Heart:** This is the *Emotional* tactic of influencing, which connects the communication or decision-making to a person's feelings of well-being or sense of belonging. You can use this tactic to appeal to the values, attitudes, ideals, and common purpose and beliefs through inspiration or enthusiasm.

3. **The Hands:** This is the *Cooperative* tactic, where you influence a person using advice, support, and offering assistance. You can reinforce your connection with this person and collaborate to accomplish a mutual goal. Here you can extend a helping hand to get the job done or for the goal to be achieved.

Depending on the person you are networking with, they all have different preferences on how they prefer being approached or how they would like to be influenced. As a networker, your most important homework for your networking plan is deciding the best influence tactic to achieve your desired outcome from a person or group of people.

You may not have the right answer immediately, especially when you do not know any of them. If this is your first time meeting them, you should be good at improvising too. Changing from one tactic to another is important, especially when you see their body language changing from being interested to being dull and bored.

To be an effective networker, it is good to know how people prefer to be influenced and apply those tactics to build commitment and alignment.

Don't worry, though—this comes with practice. You do not need to know everything on the go. The more you put yourself out there for networking, the easier it will get and the more relaxed you will be.

Six Essential Influencing Skills

Engaging the Head, Heart, and Hands effectively with different people and in different situations requires the networker to have a diverse set of skills. You need them to shape direction, commitment, and alignment with the people you speak to and network with. To pick these skills up, here is what you need to work on:

- Understanding and navigating organizational politics

  Unfortunately, politics in the workplace is unavoidable, and because all kinds of organizations have both formal and informal structures, politics of varying degrees occur. Whether you are the leader, the business owner, or the employee, you need to navigate through complex political situations. Adjusting to corporate politics comes with experience, and you should be sensitive to how the organization and its structure functions.

- Creating visibility

To create new opportunities, you need to stand out and be noticed by the people in the room but also stay authentic. Present yourself as a member of the team or part of society, talk to people, and shine, but do not over-promote yourself.

- Building and maintaining trust

  This is an extremely important element in your career and in your business—trust. With trust, you can convince people to take risks with you, but for this to happen, they should believe in you and your goals. You need to have integrity, and integrity takes time to build. Make sure when you network, you keep reminding yourself of this and do things based on your values and principles, not for the sake of doing them.

- Leveraging your networks

Networking is all about forming and nurturing relationships, and in today's interconnected world, relationships are invaluable. Through networking, you can generate new experiences and tap into the skills and visions of other people.

- Having clear communications

Part of developing persuasion skills is to communicate clearly. When you do not present your case well, persuasion falls flat. Writing and speaking clearly and briefly is imperative, and applying various kinds of communication styles will help you get your message to your target and ensure you make the right impact.

- Motivating other people

The moment you motivate people, you create a climate where they become more empowered, more engaged, and more convinced. You need to understand people's styles, their motivators, and their needs to empower them. Part of persuasion also means you need to understand their motivations and give them encouragement to pursue their goals. When you do this, people are more willing to work with you and more receptive to your influence.

Chapter 18—Developing a Confident Sense of Style

You have the skills and knowledge, you know what to say, you know who will attend your networking event, and you have a networking plan. So now what?

Now it's time to talk about your actual presence there. No, it isn't about your persona or your confidence—we talked about those things in previous chapters. It is about presenting yourself well—what you should wear to make an impact.

Paying attention to what you wear is crucial. You want to wear the right clothing or be in the right attire to fit the occasion. It shows you pay attention to rules and details because you dressed according to the invitation's guidelines. It also shows you care enough and made an effort to dress up, and we all know how the saying goes—it is always good to dress up rather than to dress down.

Ok, so maybe you have not paid attention to your style. It doesn't necessarily mean you have to follow the latest trends, but you do need to dress according to the era. A clean white shirt, a formal black dress, a pair of well-fitting pants, and a neutral tie are essentials in any wardrobe.

In this chapter, let's look at the way we style ourselves. A simple Google search or a Pinterest browse will give you image after image of what you can wear for:

- A dinner party
- A formal dinner
- A black-tie event
- A white tie event
- An auction
- A barbeque
- A social mixer
- A career fair
- An industry fair

Pinterest takes searching and browsing to a whole new level, as you can pin and make notes of what people wear so you can replicate it in your own wardrobe.

While you can create your own sense of style, you should follow certain universal style rules.

As the French say, "Bon chic, bon genre," which means *Good Style, Good Attitude.*

To dress well is to also to project a good attitude.

You may or may not have all the rules of fashion pat-down, and if you are worried or not sure where to start, always go with a classic and simple style. But for the most part, here are the essentials you want to equip your wardrobe with to achieve a simple but versatile style.

Here are a few ground rules:

1. No flashing of logos or brands

You want to project confidence and relatability. Think of a classy person you look up to in terms of style—you wouldn't see any of them carrying bags with labels emblazoned vividly. Try to avoid any flamboyant show of wealth. It's a crasser class. You can create a different experience with a brand image of your choice compared to the rest of the world. Avoid outward expressions of wealth and branded items and go with more subtle items with either a small logo or none at all.

Allow your style to speak for itself. Go for classic black laptop bags or shoulder bags to hold your things or even dark brown or mahogany bags, which go well with almost any color.

The idea is just by looking at the item of clothing, one can tell if it is an expensive brand or not without looking at a logo. All you need to do is carry it with class. For those who follow fashion trends and the latest collections, understated elegance is your best bet.

2. Neutrals are a key color palette

Colors are a personal preference for many people. Some wear bold colors while most stick with neutral colors. These bold colors are usually in the form of jewelry or a skinny scarf, shoes, bags, and other accessories.

Black, grey, ivory, white, and navy blue are favorite color palettes among business and career people. You can take fashion cues from television newscasters or real-life entrepreneurs such as Sophia Amoroso, Tory Burch, Larry Page, Bill Gates, and Mark Zuckerberg. They all have distinctive styles and prefer wearing neutral color palettes.

Businesspeople, entrepreneurs, and plenty of people on the go tend not to wear many colors, or barely any. If they do wear, it's in accessories like scarves, jewelry, ties, shoes, bags, etc.

Black plays a major role in business chic wardrobe, as it gives classic taste to any fashion piece. It is also easy to pair things easily without spending too much time figuring out what to wear. Regarding makeup for women, go for neutral and simple and keep colors to bold lips (like Alexandria Ocasio-Cortez) in a variety of red hues.

3. They follow a certain uniform of sorts

Most businesspeople technically mastered the idea of capsule wardrobes long before anyone else did. Businesspeople who embody a chic sense of style wear a basic business uniform, albeit putting their own unique take on it.

In the wardrobe of the business world, you often find skinny jeans and ballet flats or jeans with a white shirt for business casual, good sleek stilettos or a pair of black business shoes for a formal event, and maybe a fitting t-shirt and blazer or a well-fitting leather jacket for a weekend mixer.

4. Over accessorizing is a big no-no

As the greatest fashion icon, Coco Chanel, said, "Before you leave the house, look in the mirror and remove one accessory." This works for both men and women. You may think you've accessorized enough or too little, but check yourself in the mirror again. Men might have essential accessories such as a watch, a tie, or a lapel pin. Women's accessories could be earrings, a watch, a necklace, or even a tie.

While accessories create texture, over-accessorizing, on the other hand, can kill an outfit. For businesspeople, it is good to abide by the great Coco Chanel's fashion rule and always look put together, whether it's a chunky necklace, a thin tie, a statement bangle, or a classy lapel pin.

5. Save the sky-high heels or the flashy shoes for the red carpet

Or a gala dinner. Many businesspeople are rarely seen with towering, sky-high platform heels or flashy shoes while at work. You want something comfortable to last the long hours of walking, moving from one meeting room to another, speaking to people, and getting from one place to another easily. Tacky heels or shoes do not spell serious, confident, or even sexy, and no person would be caught dead in something they are not comfortable wearing in the workplace and business.

This doesn't mean women shouldn't wear heels or men shouldn't wear fashionable shoes. You need to wear the right footwear for the right event or occasion.

6. They never look uncomfortable

The last thing you want to do is look uncomfortable in the clothes you wear to a business meeting, a networking event, a conference, or even a career fair. If you are not sure what to wear, stick to wearing classic pieces that make you comfortable and make you look good. Black pants and a white shirt with a tie, a pencil skirt, and a white shirt with even ballet flats do the trick. Straight cut jeans with a plain shirt or top with a blazer are all comfortable yet professional choices. There is no point wearing tight-fitting dresses or tight-fitting shirts that restrict airflow, and neither do you want your clothing too short or too low. You can accentuate your greatest assets in a tasteful, professional, and graceful way.

Nothing is less sexy than a man or woman trying too hard to be confident or sexy or pulled together, because they will look uncomfortable. Sometimes wearing the most basic items can be professional and sexy when you feel confident and comfortable in them.

7. Always dress up rather than dress down

Casual or business casual does not mean you can waltz out of your home looking like you just grabbed the nearest thing from your closet.

Looking presentable is the goal without looking so over the top. You want to impress but not look like you took hours to decide on what to wear. The point is, you want to dress up to look presentable and casual because you never know who you will meet! Putting in extra effort to look good shows you care about what you do, the people you meet, and the event you are attending.

Make a distinction in your wardrobe between the clothes you wear at home and those you wear exclusively outside the house. The businessperson has no "day off," even if it will a beach cocktail event. No going out with pajamas; rather, you will wear real pants and shoes, and no UGG boots. Always remember you might meet someone you've wanted to meet for a long time, and first impressions count.

8. The makeup

While more women wear makeup than men, let's face it, it's 2019, and it is not a big deal to wear makeup even if you are a guy. Regarding wearing makeup in business, minimalism is your best friend for both a woman and a man. French chic makeup is a good option because it usually focuses on one bold item. It's either a good eye makeup with a neutral lip, a bold red lip with neutral eyes, or on most days, a well-lined eye with soft blush and nude lips. French chic makeup is not a heavily made-up look. It is a subtle mix of the bold and the minimal.

Sometimes they wear minimal makeup, such as a lip gloss with lightly brushed mascara and a soft dab of blush. Lipstick and mascara seem to be the most commonly worn items by the French women and they, like the Koreans, do not cover up their skin to airbrushed perfection.

The average businessperson or entrepreneur should go with a clean, minimal make-up or clean-shaven face and not cake on make-up with obvious contouring of the skin, unkempt beard, and oily hair.

Now we have covered the basic essentials and style guidelines of what it means to a business professional yet stylish, so here are some outfit choices you can try your hand at:

Outfit choices for the average entrepreneur:

• The Casually Polished Look Outfit

The casually polished look usually encompasses neutral colors from beige to nude. Sometimes it can be totally black, but more often you will see many career people with a simple and crisp white dinner jacket with a statement tee underneath for a pop of color. Often this look is paired with nude shoes or ballet flats and aviators and dark jeans or skinny jeans. A scarf is usually in a bold color if not the crossbody bag.

- The Working Day Outfit

The working chic outfit usually has black in it and sometimes, 100 percent black from the head to the toes. Three-inch Mary Janes for women or court shoes for men complete the pants, skirt, and sweater look, with a black clutch or black laptop bag tucked underneath the arm and a pair of sunglasses for a cool look. The one thing that pops could be a gorgeous red lip for the women or a brown shoe for men, together with a pair of simple pearl stud earrings for women or a belt for the man.

This look is minimal, yet the different textures pull the entire outfit together without looking too prim and proper.

The working chic outfit can also have a leather jacket either in tan or black to make this otherwise conservative look a little toughened up. Hair can be swept into a simple ponytail for women and combed for men.

- The mother or father of three outfit

Forget about those stereotype mom or dad images you often see in commercials, usually filled with moms and dads in button-up shirts and three-quarter pants. The business chic mother has her hair either loosely plaited in a braid or in a messy bun with deep red lips. A light touch of mascara gives an effortless and comfortable look. The business chic dad has a plaid shirt under a navy-blue sweater with a pair of beige corduroy pants and comfortable loafers.

This simple look is easy to pull together when you are a mother or father of three young children because it is effortless. You can pair up comfortable white jeans with an off-shoulder tee and a slight silver chain running down for an elongated look or a pair of jeans with a simple shirt and a nice pair of shoes to tie the whole look together.

- The "coffee with your friends" outfit

Another pulled-together black outfit except for the touch of color came from their bright accessories such as the tie, scarf, or a belt. Again, this ensemble, while minimal, looks extremely comfortable yet stylish. This look can be liberating and paired with well-fitted biker boots; you can have coffee and head to a bar when night falls.

Conclusion

Since we have some insight into the business chic mindset and a few examples of outfit ensembles, here is a concluded list of wardrobe essentials you can acquire to dress chic and stylish for a business event.

These items work well for any season, but you should add certain pieces to your wardrobe to showcase your own personal style.

Depending on what the weather is like where you live, you may also want to add some winter boots and a good winter jacket to your wardrobe.

Otherwise, this list covers most of the basics you need for the entire year

The Ideal Business Wardrobe:

BLAZERS/JACKETS/TOPPERS

- White blazer — A tuxedo or dinner-style jacket

- Black blazer — Always an essential in any wardrobe you create

- Black leather jacket — How about making this brown or tan rather than black?

- Mixed tweed/leather jacket —This jacket makes for a dressy and a casual look depending on how you style them.

SWEATERS

- Navy sweater — A must in any wardrobe
- Camel sweater — Another essential item in a neutral tone
- Black turtleneck — preferably cowled or thick neck or in thin knit

SHIRTS/TOPS

- Fitted black t-shirt —Never go wrong
- Fitted white t-shirt — Must have always
- White draped t-shirt — A loose t-shirt in grey, navy, or black or any other neutral color works wonders
- Navy-patterned tank top
- Graphic grey tank top — For casual pairings with jeans and other pants
- Plain grey tank top
- Striped navy-blue long-sleeved shirt
- White long-sleeved shirt

PANTS

- Black skinny jeans
- Black straight cut jeans
- Dark denim jeans — Either in boot-cut or skinny or even straight-legged
- Black trousers —Classy, thin trousers
- Tailored black or beige pants

SKIRTS

- Black pencil skirt – Well-fitted, absolute must-have

- Flared black skirt — To add another layer of texture and dimension

DRESSES

- Casual grey summer dress in a pinstripe
- Black sheath dress
- Bold summer dress

COAT

- Autumn or winter wool coat in a neutral color

SHOES/HEELS/BOOTS

- Leather sandals
- Ballet flats
- Black pumps in a chic, classy, manageable height
- Tall leather boots
- Short biker boots
- Loafers
- White sneakers
- Black shoes

PURSES

- Black clutch
- Casual satchel bag
- Structured bag
- Sturdy laptop bag

ACCESSORIES

- Simple minimalist watch
- Sunglasses

- Gloves

- Circle scarf

- A fun patterned scarf

- A bright scarf

- Pearl studs

- Dangly earrings

- Delicate necklace with a small pendant

- Layered chain necklaces (in gold and silver)

Et voilà! With these essentials, you can mix and match to your heart's desire, and you will have plenty of outfit choices for the entire year, whether it is winter, spring, summer, or autumn. Just remember to keep it simple, adding a pop of color either in your makeup or accessories.

Style is a personal preference. If you don't normally put much thought into how you dress, then the safest way to go is to be minimalistic in your choices. Keep colors to neutral black, white, or navy blue and make sure your clothing choices are simple, yet clean and up to date. Don't keep a 90s style long pants just because you can still fit it, but it looks out of date. If you want to go with the vintage look, then make sure you know how to pull it off.

Hygiene is also a must. Make sure your face is clean and you shower and shave so you look clean and presentable at all times. Looking gruff like Matthew McConaughey or having an out-of-bed look a la Serena van der Woodsen on Gossip Girls will not work if you do not look pulled together or clean. Also, wear minimal deodorant and perfume.

Remember to stay simple and comfortable for your business meetings and networking events, no matter what kind they are, because you never know who you will meet. First impressions count!

Chapter 19—Using the Right Words to Connect with People

In the age of instant communication, it is much easier to speak to people, no matter who they are. You can simultaneously "speak" to several people at different times; for example, you can be typing an email and speaking to a friend on Skype, sending a message on WhatsApp, and also talking to your colleague next to you.

How effective are these communications, and did you address the issues presented during these communication periods, answer the questions, and give the proper solutions to all these interlocutors?

It is important to keep in mind technology should be used to create effective dialogues. If you are open to communication coming from the minds of other people, then you can create meaning and purpose from virtual encounters through effortless technology.

Therefore, it is imperative to be personally engaged and to effectively listen to what others have to say when you navigate the frenzy of technology and non-technology interlocutors.

Regarding networking with people, most networking scenarios take place offline rather than online. So what can you say to connect with your person? What can you do to make them feel you empathize with them?

Saying the right things at the right time is important because it can make or break your conversation with them. One of the first things you want to do is empathize with them and see things from their point of view.

So how do you do that? Here are some words you can use when you converse with people:

- I totally understand.

People have a strong desire to connect and to hear "Yes, I understand" warms the heart of the people involved in the process of communication. People want to know if their message is understood and they are not alone in their thinking. To understand and acknowledge another person's point of view is the first step in understanding and creating the basis of successful communication. It makes both parties feel connected and reassured. The act of being present during the moment of communication means you need to give focused attention to what the other person is saying. By paying total attention to your interlocutor, they will feel more empowered and acknowledged.

- Great, tell me more about it.

This sentence signals to the other person that you are indeed curious and interested in what they have to say. Use this phrase to prioritize the dialogue, either by being silently focused or intently focusing by asking the necessary questions.

- What do you think?

This is a powerful question because it recognizes your interlocutor's subject expertise. When you ask this question, you create a space that enables authentic suggestion from the other person. You must be aware of the interests, ideas, and thoughts of the other person's; their suggestion should be genuine, and you must be open to accepting these suggestions; otherwise, you open another line of disagreement, waste both people's time, and build frustration.

- I see where you are coming from.

This sentence is powerful, and it signals to the other person your willingness to engage actively in what they are saying. When rephrasing what the other person has just formulated, you contribute to the communication flow by clarifying your own understanding of the issue, and you open up the possibility of getting more details. When you say this sentence, it benefits both interlocutors as your conversation swiftly moves into a common meaning.

- You are right.

When this is said, people automatically feel they have been praised positively, especially when said with sincerity. Saying you are wrong and they are right is also a way of showing you are a humble communicator and a person your employees can identify with. People are more open and trusting with those they can identify with. Telling someone they are right will create common ground and move toward solutionizing.

- I trust your judgment.

Trust combines both competence and character. Character refers to who you are as a person, whereas competence refers to what you can do effectively. Competence varies based on the contexts. Telling your partner or employee you trust them is meaningful, so say it when you mean it. When you tell someone you trust their judgment, this means you believe in their capabilities and you also acknowledge their competencies. This will lead them to feel more motivated to actively contribute to the project and give more creative ideas.

- I don't know.

Nobody has the answers to everything and acknowledging you do not know something means you are humble but also courageous. Saying I don't know followed by a willingness to seek answers and solutions can start up a dialogue and bond the people in a group toward common goals. You can also say, "I'm not sure, but I will find out" or "I will think about it." This tells the other person you value their input and will consider the options and exercise your authority to make the right decisions. This will give you time to figure out the right solution, and your interlocutors will also see you as flexible and open-minded.

- Thank you.

This shows the person you appreciate their time and investment in the conversation. It also exudes sincerity and is the most basic code of social etiquette. In a professional environment, this shows you are open to engaging politely with your team. *Please* is also another important word in communication, and sometimes we forget to say these words in the complexity of daily life. But remember to keep practicing saying please and thank you simply because it enables people to be more willing participants in the project.

- Well done.

Saying this also creates a certain warmth in the relationship between two people. It does wonders for your communication and social skills because people want to know if their idea was great and usable. If you are in a place of authority, this will enable people to work better with you as they see you as someone who appreciates good and workable ideas. They would also be more open to constructive feedback when you give praise where it is due.

- I'm on it.

This powerful display of expression is an extremely empathic one. When you say this, the person on the receiving end knows you are committed to seeing the idea through, and it also shows you care about the project. You can also quickly win the confidence of your collaborators and partners because you have displayed a willingness to commit. When you say this, make sure you are authentic in your commitment, and you want to make it happen, no matter what it takes.

These sentences help improve your communication style when speaking to a person or a group of people. It also enables you to have a positive outlook and influence on their lives and helps build better relationships, especially when you have to network with plenty of people in the same event. A little manners and ethics will definitely take you a long way and create a positive impression on the people you speak to.

Conclusion

We've come to the end of the book, and we hope you've gained enough information to help you kick-start a successful networking journey!

A successful networking venture involves:

- Understanding what networking is all about
- Knowing the kinds or types of events people usually organize for networking
- Creating your own networking plan
- Working on your charisma, confidence, and personality

Everything else, such as building your small talk capabilities, understanding body language, and developing emotional intelligence comes with practice. The more you get involved in events, open yourself up to people, talk about a variety of topics, and break out of your shell, the better you'll be in reading the signs and signals that lead to successful small talks. The more well-versed you become in turning small talks into conversations, the more confident you will be.

Along the way, you will also use better persuasion and negotiating skills to get your idea across and increase buy-in from the people you connect with. Networking, after all, is a combination of these factors put into practice to ensure a sustainable and successful outcome.

Remember it is alright to feel anxious or worried before meeting new people or people you've held in high esteem. It's part of being human. That said, you must not let these negative emotions overcome you and destroy all the things you've been preparing yourself for. Therefore, developing a positive mindset is crucial so you can use positive affirmations to fight back negative thoughts each time you are getting too pessimistic.

Using the right words at the right time also helps greatly in ensuring you do not cross ethical or cultural boundaries when talking to people of different cultures or age groups.

All the above should be packaged decently, which is why dressing right is also essential—never forget because how you dress creates the first impressions people form of you. When you look clean and put together, people are more open to talking to you and forming a conversation.

All set to network? Good luck, and we hope you achieve all your targeted goals in your business and career!

Check out another book by Mark Dudley

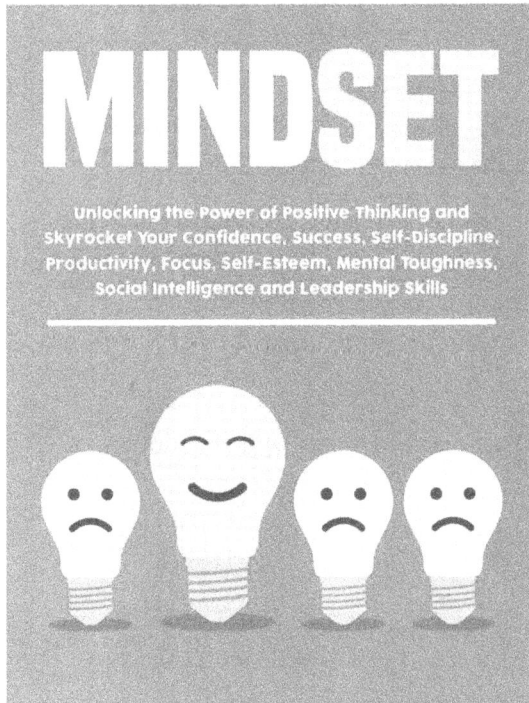

MINDSET

Unlocking the Power of Positive Thinking and Skyrocket Your Confidence, Success, Self-Discipline, Productivity, Focus, Self-Esteem, Mental Toughness, Social Intelligence and Leadership Skills

MARK DUDLEY

You might like this one as well

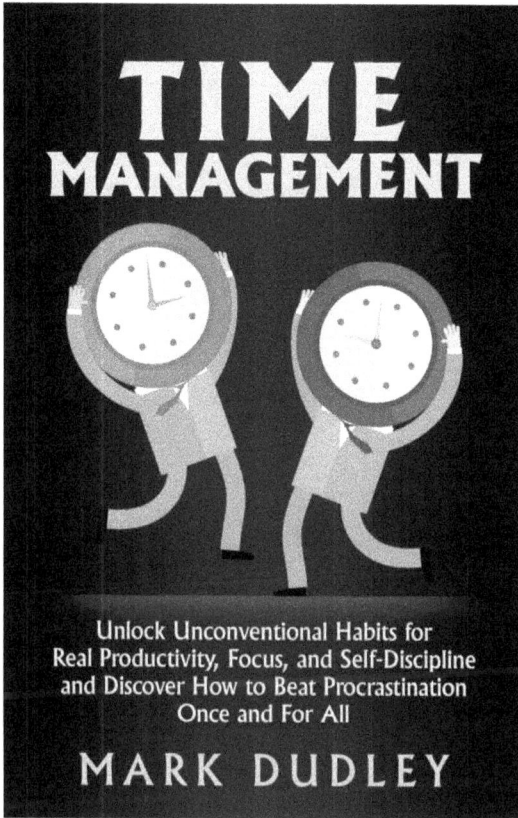

TIME
MANAGEMENT

Unlock Unconventional Habits for
Real Productivity, Focus, and Self-Discipline
and Discover How to Beat Procrastination
Once and For All

MARK DUDLEY

www.ingramcontent.com/pod-product-compliance
Lightning Source LLC
Chambersburg PA
CBHW071955260326
41914CB00004B/803